~ SISTER ~
WENDY's
Odyssey

On the odyssey I left my solitude and went out to
six great art collections, hoping that seeing face-to-face what I
had seen only in reproduction would be a great delight that I
could share with others.

~ SISTER ~
WENDY's
Odyssey

A Journey of
Artistic Discovery

~

SISTER WENDY BECKETT

BBC BOOKS

This book is dedicated to Nick Rossiter and John Hooper,
my dear friends,
to Heather McCubbin and Ben Fox,
to Toby Eady,
and to all the cameramen, soundmen and other professionals
who were so patient with my inexperience.

~

This book is published to accompany the
television series *Sister Wendy's Odyssey*
which was first broadcast in 1992.

Published by BBC Books,
a division of BBC Enterprises Limited,
Woodlands, 80 Wood Lane
London W12 0TT.

First published 1993
© Sister Wendy Beckett 1993
ISBN 0 563 36957 4

Designed by Barbara Mercer
Photographs on pages 12, 26, 38, 50, 62 and 74 by Chris Andrews, Oxford Picture Library
Photographs on pages i, iii and 86 by Justin Pumfrey
Set in Spectrum by Selwood Systems, Midsomer Norton
Printed and bound in Great Britain by Butler & Tanner Ltd, Frome & London
Colour separation by Technik Ltd, Berkhamsted
Jacket printed by Lawrence Allen Ltd, Weston-super-Mare

CONTENTS

~

INTRODUCTION

Making the odyssey, my journey to six places in Britain to visit art collections, was difficult in practice but simple in essence. I knew where I wanted to go and what I wanted to do and it was really a matter of bending all my energies towards achieving this. But after the odyssey, people began to ask me questions and I found this much more complex. They were questions about myself which, I am sure foolishly, I had not expected and questions about art and my desire to share it, which is not always easy to explain. But I tried to answer these questions and here is the gist of what I was asked and what I replied.

The first question was often about my desire to be a nun: when did I come to realize this longing? In fact, I cannot remember a time when it was not clear to me that this is what I wanted, so I never had a great disclosure scene with my parents. They accepted from early on that, nuisance of a child though I was, I still wanted passionately to belong wholly to God.

I was not yet seventeen when I left home to join the Sisters with whom I spent my last years at school: the Sisters of Nôtre Dame. Nowadays we would not allow a girl so young to enter a convent. We would insist that she finish her education, get a job, learn about the world. For me, though, it was completely right. The only disadvantage in entering a convent so young — though paradoxically this very disadvantage later proved to be a blessing — was that I was too stupid a sixteen-year-old to realize that in joining a teaching order I was putting myself into a position where I would have to teach.

I had never wanted to teach: what I wanted was to pray, but I could also see that making a vow of obedience meant giving oneself to God, and that entailed trusting Him and not opting out when I did not like what I was asked to do. So I taught for about sixteen years, waiting confidently for the day when God would arrange for me to lead a contemplative life, and He did! Of course, God does not jiggle the strings to make things happen. His arrangement came about, as such things usually do, through the course of nature. (We pray not to have the course of nature changed but to be helped to see in that course what God intends for us and to use it to grow in love and joy.) I became ill and I was no longer able to teach properly and finally the Notre Dame nuns, generously and solicitously, said that they thought I had been right in saying I needed to lead a life of prayer. They could see that it was not just that I wanted it, but that I truly needed it, and so they arranged for me to come to the monastery.

I find that it is not unusual for people to think they would like to live in solitude, but in fact they are really thinking how nice it would be to escape from all the demands of life, from jobs and bills and family worries and relationship problems, from adult responsibilities. This is a serious danger. If one is to take solitude seriously as a lifetime vocation, then there must not be in it this element of escape. The normal means of becoming holy is through living with other people. That is how we are meant to be purified, learning to become unselfish by the sheer pressure of duty and of love. So I am taking a great risk in trusting that God will purify me when I am leading a life that could in theory be a selfish life. I have to take my vocation with the utmost responsibility and beg God to let me live here unselfishly, not for my own sake but for others. My trust is that I shall receive from direct contact with God what other people – more balanced, brave and normal people – receive from living a normal life. It is not because I am better that I live in solitude but because I am beneath the usual standard, unable to sustain the normal human burdens. So I have to be very honest in accepting with love the burdens of the solitary life, and not cheat!

The life of prayer depends completely on believing in the value of prayer. It is a total act of faith, because there is no concrete result to show the world. One does not live a life of prayer for oneself, one lives it wholly so as to receive God's love and compassion and somehow pour it out on the world's pain. There is so much suffering in the world and I am totally convinced that praying for people, not by name but just with open-ended love, will help change their attitudes. If our attitudes change, then what we have to suffer becomes more bearable. We have a thrifty God, who wants nothing in our lives to be useless or wasted. But suffering is very difficult to make fruitful, and the contemplative life is based resolutely upon the certainty that profound prayer makes God's love and compassion and warmth present in our moral atmosphere – invisibly, intangibly but truly. Of course, you need corporeal acts of charity also: you need Mother Theresa's nuns to bring bodily healing and teaching orders like Notre Dame to bring mental enlightenment, so that we are helped to become whole in mind and body. But we also need contemplative nuns to make present an attitude of spirit that will bring us to inner peace.

From its very nature, the life of prayer demands asceticism so that everything in it is geared to setting you free for God. It is this spiritual freedom that matters, not suffering for the sake of suffering, which is useless. God takes no pleasure in anybody making their life physically or morally miserable. The aim is for everything in life to work, to be functional, to set you free to look at God and draw His compassionate gaze down upon the sufferings of the world. There has to be a balance between living a sparse life and living one so physically hard that it actually impedes prayer by making one think about oneself. We want to forget ourselves and just look lovingly at God.

My life may sound hard but, by the grace of God, it is not especially difficult. (My mother once said to my sister: 'Poor Wendy, she has such a hard life', to which my sister robustly replied: 'Poor Wendy nothing, she's doing exactly what she wants to do!') I get up at three every morning because I spend seven hours or so in prayer a day, and I like to get a good start in the silence. Then at about five I leave the caravan for the only time during the day and go up to the monastery to join the community for morning prayer. I wait there until it is eight and time for Holy Mass. After Mass I get my basket from the Sisters with my day's provisions and go back to the caravan where I shall be alone for the rest of the day, finishing my seven hours of prayer, doing about two hours of work, reading, perhaps walking a little, thinking, looking at art, trying to be completely surrendered to God, with no thought for the narrowness of self but taking in the great expanse of God's beauty. Then around eight it is time to lie down and see if I sleep or merely lie there resting in peace. (Notice that I get as much sleep as most people, possibly more, but it is at an unusual time.)

My love for art is for me a way of loving God. I do not usually speak of Him explicitly since religious language can sometimes put people off. But art is essentially beauty that draws us into the truth of our own being, and whenever we have truth and beauty we have God. This does not have to be spelt out: it simply happens. For me, it even seems that art can expose parts of the self I was not aware of, so there is more of me laid bare for God to possess. Art is a way of making me human, and you cannot pray unless you are rooted in the truth of your own humanity. Prayer is never an escape but the opposite, an exposure. The real self is held out to the real God, and any pretence or lack of reality makes the whole exercise futile.

Everything in life is a means to an end, and the end for me is always God. In that sense, art is also a means to an end, but that is not simply to use it to illustrate religious beliefs. Art exists, whatever uses are made of it, and just in existing it proclaims truth. Religious art is just one of the ways it can be used; it is sometimes used to make political points, too. But art need have no religious or political angle. All great art, through its own nature, takes us beyond what we hold already in our thoughts, and opens up a new experience.

I have been asked if I see any contradiction between my contemplative life and the public role of art critic, but the question rather baffles me. Thinking, writing or talking about art normally occupies a very small part of my time. This last year (1992) has been a hard one in that making the television series took me away so much, but I feel that it was asked of me and that it would have been selfish of me not to do it. In fact, the very difficulties of having to be away from the silence of the caravan are an asset, perhaps purifying away a little more of my deep selfishness. If one became bored with silence and solitude and actively sought to go out, one would be in danger. Intellectually, I can see that there could be a desire for any diversion which would get one away from the sheer pressure of nothing but God, which is a great joy and a great pain simultaneously, but it is a temptation from which I have been mercifully spared. Solitude is a gift so precious that only the desire to respond to what God seems to be asking makes it possible to leave it for a time.

I leave it, with a wrench, but contentedly, because I am seeking to share what I find in art, its deep enrichment of the spirit. Art is only great if it draws you down into the depths of your being and exposes you to the truth of what you are and what you could become. Any art that does that, no matter what its theme, is spiritual, a deepening of our truth. Art is for everybody; all we need is to give it time. We sometimes want to say, after a quick glance, that we do not like what we are looking at. But it took the artist time to make it: it takes us time to see it. We have to let the work affect us, take us out of our preconceptions into someone else's world. As well as time, this needs some humility and an open mind: what it does not need is education. The woman in the supermarket is perhaps better prepared to experience art than the scholar in his ivory tower who might be cut off from the work by arrogance. The woman in the supermarket or that perpetual man in the street have their own human truth, and that is enough. Take me, for example. In many ways I am an inadequate person. I am completely uncreative: I am no good at cooking or sewing or gardening, let alone painting. I have no gifts, yet I am lit up by the wonder of what I see. I am taught about pain and joy, and if a limited person like me can receive this enrichment, so can anybody!

Even those who, like me, cannot very often visit art galleries can gain an immense amount from reproductions, looking at postcards or books at home or perhaps in a library. Obviously you have to make an imaginative leap to experience the size and the texture which the reproduction cannot give you, but this has its own advantages. It makes you look with concentrated attention, and the attention can be all on the art rather than on the gallery and the other people and the images on either side ... The great essential for art appreciation is said to be a chair: very true!

Sometimes I have been asked if I do not over-emphasize the spiritual in art. If I do, it is through personal clumsiness, because I am not waving a solo banner here. There are many people who think that art is spiritual, so much so that the word is becoming overworked. I believe I am voicing what many think, and many are voicing it more powerfully than I am. Art is something of enormous value, and more and more people are describing that value as spiritual. Perhaps it is better not to say so unless the nature of the work absolutely demands it.

Here is where my being a nun works against me in some minds. Yet nuns are a cross-section of humanity and there are no labels that tie a nun down to being a special kind of person. It seems very narrow-minded to hold her vocation against somebody. Ah, people say, but a nun can know nothing of life! True, I have been very sheltered, but I have had the great blessing of being able to read. Once you can read, all worlds are open to you. Think of Jane Austen who lived all her life as a quiet spinster lady with her mother and sister, yet her reading and thinking enabled her to know the human heart through and through. A great novel takes you deep into the wonders and complexities of other lives, making you free of reality. Experience is a tricky affair: it is the imagination and the spirit that matter, not the material circumstances. Writers are always jibing at Shakespeare's apparently rather circumscribed life and claiming for him all sorts of adventures from which he wrote his dramas. But this may not be true, and is certainly not necessary. The heart, contemplating the tragedies and comedies of life, can take us infinitely far.

On the odyssey I left my solitude and went out to six great art collections, hoping that seeing face-to-face what I had seen only in reproduction would be a great delight that I could share with others.

Walker Art Gallery

LIVERPOOL

My journey was an odyssey only in the humblest sense, yet I did, like Odysseus, go to strange places and see wonderful things. I was determined not to include London in my travels because we all know there are marvellous art galleries there and I wanted to show that there is equally great art in unexpected places: Aberdeen and Southampton, for example, both have splendid municipal galleries. It was very hard to decide where to go. Should it be the Orkneys, where there is a small choice collection at Stromness, all picked by the unerring eye of one great collector, Margaret Gardiner? Or should it be the strange rococo meringue of the Bowes Museum at Barnard Castle, likewise the choice of the Bowes family, who felt they were rather rash in paying out a whole eight pounds for their marvellous El Greco? Or Walsall Museum, with its unique Epsteins and African art? However, one of my six places was always going to be Liverpool. It has superb museums, such as the Merseyside County Museum, which houses one of the greatest collections of medieval ivories in the world, not to mention five hundred classical sculptures and rare Anglo-Saxon jewellery. The Sudley Art Gallery is an early Victorian merchant's house, with a fine Turner and a Constable, and there is the University Art Gallery too, with another exceptional Turner and modern sculpture by Barbara Hepworth and Phillip King. But the one work above all that drew me to Liverpool was in the Walker Art Gallery, where the collection ranges from early Italian and Netherlandish art right up to the present.

What I longed to see was a masterwork by the early Sienese painter Simone Martini. But I knew that the Martini was only foremost among many others there, such as Guercino's contemplations on the biblical stories and Poussin's on the myths. I had not really intended to visit the Tate of the North, but an exhibition of Stanley Spencer's work was in progress while I was there, and I could not resist the chance to decide for myself whether he was or was not the greatest religious painter of our century. I sat and looked, I walked around and pondered, but I still had to come away defeated. Defeats in art appreciation, though, are also victories, because we go on thinking and looking and, as we do, our understanding grows. It is the journey we make that matters, not the arrival at the haven of a settled opinion.

Christ Discovered in the Temple

Simone Martini

Born Siena, Italy c.1284
Died probably at Avignon, France 1344

~

When they have an exceptional and rare masterpiece, some museums isolate it so that its significance is apparent. The Louvre does this with the *Mona Lisa* and the Prado with Velázquez' *Las Meninas*. But the Walker Art Gallery takes its jewel-like Simone Martini, small and uniquely beautiful, and hangs it humbly on the wall among its fellow fourteenth-century Italian works. If we stand transfixed before it, it is because the painting has stopped us by the sheer impact of its quality. Simone Martini manages to unite two extremes: the utmost elegance and grace with an earthy human realism. Here he is showing us, in brilliant colour and formal subtlety, the generation gap.

Mary sits at one side of the panel, Jesus stands at the other. Each is bewildered. Mary and Joseph are hurt and astonished that their child had left them for three days without word of his whereabouts. Jesus is hurt and astonished that they did not realize that he would be in the Temple, his 'Father's house'. Poor St Joseph tries ineffectively to restore harmony between them. Martini shows us a daringly truculent Child Jesus and is equally daring in his admonishing Mother Mary. He is depicting, delicately and soberly, that moment in everyone's life when we experience the shock of misunderstanding from those we love.

When we are young, we take it for granted that others think as we do, and it is a painful awakening into adult reality to discover that we may love and be loved and still not understand or be understood. Even in the Holy Family, this mutual incomprehension is natural and Martini shows us both child and mother struggling to come to terms with it. Eyes lock on to one another with stony force, hands are withdrawn or extended admonishingly. Martini is the great virtuoso of body language. But he softens the impact of the conflict by the glory of his colour and the dancing sweetness of his line. He further reassures us by the gold background. This event is not literally happening as he shows it to us. He does not set it in the actual Temple but in some ethereal no-place where the most painful emotions are resolved under the calming glow of the golden atmosphere, symbolic of heaven. Mary's cloak froths around her feet like a gleaming wave, and Joseph's upper garment tightens into almost abstract patterns of creases, pale and luminous purple behind Mary's rich blue and the scarlet, blue and gold of the Child.

This is such a witty picture, despite its seriousness, with the man who matters least in the story given the central position, lost in the drama, earnestly trying to reconcile what cannot be reconciled: two different ways of looking at the world, which remain individual no matter how much they share the same principles.

Christel Discovered in the Temple   **Simone Martini**   **1342**
Tempera on panel   49.6 × 35.1cm (19½ × 13¾in)
Walker Art Gallery, Liverpool

I must confess I have a passion for Poussin, that most intellectual painter whose thinking is suffused by the most intense emotion. This is one of his greatest works telling one of the supreme love stories of antiquity.

Phocion was an Athenian general who was unjustly condemned to death for losing a battle. Worse than that, he was condemned to be burnt and his ashes scattered, which meant, for an Athenian, that his spirit could never rest since his body was not buried. His widow could not bear that he should have to suffer this punishment and came secretly, risking death, to collect his ashes. Then she could put them in water and swallow them and Phocion would have a tomb, a living tomb: her own body.

Poussin shows us the majestic landscape of the classical world, where all is order and dignity. The temple rises in perpendicular power, surrounded by the severe stateliness of masculine architectural authority. Even the great trees are disciplined and regular. The world moves quietly about the important affairs of commerce and law, taking no heed of the injustice done to a loser. Phocion's wife, whose very name is forgotten, crouches to her loving task in the foreground, light gleaming on her downcast head and eager arms. Her companion is clearly ter-rified, keeping an anxious look-out for observers, but the widow is solely concentrated on what she has set her heart on doing: giving her husband immortality. Her humble but passionate activity in the earth is in painful contrast to the clear calm of the background: the high and barren mountain, the noonday torpor of the passers-by, the motionless trees and the distant cloud-shadowed sky.

In its superb organization, Poussin brings before us the antithesis between the womanly world of the heart, of individual conscience, and the abstract rigour of government. There is no flexibility in this background, only the weight and power of the state at its most emphatic. As far as the horizon we see the silhouetted world of communal order, obviously a great and necessary achievement. In the foreground we see a demonstration of individual freedom. Both are needed: the lonely human being seeking what is right, at all costs, and understanding that rightness from within; and the apparatus of the state, upholding the social norms. It is when they clash that we are in danger, and Poussin gives full force to both: the fixed, immutable structure of the mind and the soft sensitive reactions of the heart. He holds them in lovely equilibrium.

Landscape with the Ashes of Phocion **Nicolas Poussin** **c.1648**
Oil on canvas   116.5 × 178.5cm (45⅞ × 70¼in)
Walker Art Gallery, Liverpool

St John the Baptist Visited in Prison by Salome

Guercino (Giovanni Barbieri)

Born Cento, near Ferrara, Italy 1591
Died Bologna, Italy 1666

~

Guercino's real name was Giovanni Francesco Barbieri, but he was known as Guercino, 'Squint-eyed'. However horrendous his squint may have been, he saw straighter than most people.

Countless Renaissance artists were fascinated by the story of Salome, the dancing girl who demanded as her reward the head of John the Baptist on a dish. But no artist except Guercino has ever gone back to the mystery of exactly why she should want that head on a dish. Here we see Guercino's guess. She loved him, she hankered for him, but he rejected her. So here is one mystery, that someone can long passionately for another and that other repulse them with implacable force. This may not seem to us a very saintly attitude, but clearly John sees Salome as temptation, the 'other' who is evil. He sets his will totally against the girl herself and all that she can offer.

The other mystery which Guercino sets before us so superbly is that of freedom. Who is really in prison here? Is it John, chained by his wrists, incarcerated in a small cell with only a cloak to wrap round him? Or is it Princess Salome, with her fine clothes and apparent liberty and her palace behind her, yet with her hand gripping so fiercely the bars of the cage? She is literally outside the prison, but spiritually she is shut up within it, in a prison of her own desires. Look at the hands: his so free, so relaxed, so at peace; hers so clenched, so tight, so urgent. A great wave of yearning goes out from her and breaks hopelessly against the rock of John's denial. Does she love him, truly? Or is it just a lust to possess, the passion of a spoilt girl who has never been denied anything and certainly never denied herself? Look too at the witty way in which Guercino makes us wonder who is really beheaded in this story: by showing only her head, he makes it look as if it is Salome. The painting tell us she has 'lost her head' in a mad desire for something she can never possess.

That is the deepest meaning of the picture: where is true freedom? Does self-will imprison us far more cruelly than stone walls and bars could ever do? There is, of course, an implied judgement, yet there is also compassion. A squinter looks at things obliquely, and the painter feels pity for the silly little rich girl. Her fleshy face makes an ironic contrast to the ascetic nobility of the captive John. We can see that there is only disaster ahead, and we grieve for both the saint and the foolish young sinner.

St John the Baptist Visited in Prison by Salome **Guercino** **c.1624–6**
Oil on canvas   81 × 97.5cm (31⅞ × 38⅜in)
Walker Art Gallery, Liverpool (temporarily loaned by the National Gallery from the collection of Sir Denis Mahon,
now returned)

I have not actually met many artists, but the first artist I did meet was Dhruva Mistry. He was having an exhibition at Cambridge of his *Guardian Figures*, and I am afraid he must have thought me very odd because to hold the hand of a real live artist brought tears to my eyes. He looked at me, I recall, with a sort of gentlemanly horror.

His *Guardian Figures* were very large, and this bull is small, but it is large in its inner majesty. Mistry has cleverly called it *Sitting Bull*, the name of one of the heroic Red Indian chiefs. This refers obliquely to Mistry's own nationality — not 'red' Indian but real Indian — and also to the nature of this animal: he is a chieftain bull, a bull of power.

Hindu culture has always recognized the divine in the animal world: there is an elephant god and a monkey god, and all cows are sacred. This little bull has an innate divinity, not in the strictly religious sense that only carries a weight of meaning for the Hindu, but in a natural sense. He is an icon, a symbol of calm and peace, of power and benignity. Mistry has sculpted him with the most tender attentiveness. He has decorated the ears with intricate care, and coiled the horns with a flourish of splendour. We can walk all round the bull, delighting in the curve of its flanks, the solidity of its rump, the precious testicles gently resting on the pedestal. Divinities are fecund, life-inspiring and life-bestowing, and the bull is alive with this kind of fruitfulness.

Like Mistry's big figures, this too is a guardian. It protects us by its very presence, and it is no lack of love for my own religious tradition that makes me say that *Sitting Bull* is not an inadequate image of the invisible God. The bull is gentle, peaceful, kindly, strong. It inspires affection and trust. Since God is essentially mysterious, is a representation such as this perhaps less harmful than some of the Old Testament images that make God seem fearsome and liable to anger? Whether we agree or not on this theological point, we can all agree on the beauty of this sculpture, and take a simple pleasure in its innocent dignity. Here is majestic mildness, so attractive that one longs to caress its flanks and run a loving hand over its head. Is it perhaps only word-play to point out that here is an artist whose very name is, in sound at least, 'mystery', and that there is a pervasive sense of precisely this in all his works?

Sitting Bull **Dhruva Mistry** **1983**
Plaster with yellow ochre polychromy 31 × 39.5 × 23.5cm (12¼ × 15½ × 9¼in)
Walker Art Gallery, Liverpool

The title of this picture, *Peter Getting Out of Nick's Pool*, is a very personal one, and to me that is an indication of why it is one of David Hockney's best. Hockney is always at his finest when he is dealing with things that really matter to him, and Nick and Peter were among his closest friends. Artists can only paint things that are central to themselves, and it is a wonderful moment in any artist's life when he or she discovers what those central things are. It would be useless for Hockney to decide, for the loftiest political reasons, to paint something like dole queues in Bradford in the rain, because intention is not enough to carry a work to a triumphant conclusion.

Here Hockney is indeed triumphant since this picture shows three things that are all important to him. He loves painting water just moving gently, stirred by a human presence: notice how brilliantly and simply he suggests this slow ripple. He loves painting sunlight, especially when it is shining with unimpeded brightness in California, spotlighting the bare, simple architecture with its implications of an ordered and stable world, something very dear to Hockney. Finally, he loves painting beautiful young men. Here the young man appears like one of those Greek statues of a youth almost more than human, frozen in a timeless world of never-ending grace. The combination of these three elements that the artist cares so passionately about enables him to make them visible to us with such lucidity.

I must confess that I am not myself a great fan of Hockney's. It is not easy to explain my lack of absolute enthusiasm, because certainly this is a splendid piece of work. Perhaps I find it a little too diagrammatic, as if he has the world so intellectually ordered that I cannot respond to it as the real world. Yet I would hate to end on a note of hesitation. If to me this is a fine painting of a fantasy world without what I consider poetry, it is not seen as such by many others. Do we perhaps all have to acknowledge certain temperamental limitations in our response to art? The fatal error would be to make up our minds quickly and then think that our own opinion is the only right one. Art, like poetry, is economical, doing many things at the same time, not contradicting but complementing one another. If only my intellect responds to the Hockney, not my heart, that is my own deficiency, not the artist's.

Peter Getting Out of Nick's Pool   **David Hockney**   **1966**
Acrylic on canvas   152 × 152cm (59⅞ × 59⅞in)
Walker Art Gallery, Liverpool

I find it difficult to make up my mind about Stanley Spencer. He has been hailed as the greatest religious artist in Britain, and about that I have great doubts. In fact, I totally disagree, as to me his religion appears self-centred and relatively superficial. Many also claim that he is the greatest British artist of our century, and there too I have niggling doubts. This is in no sense a religious picture, but it is a very strong picture, painted out of deep emotion and with enormous skill. That I admit unhesitatingly. Certain parts of it are wonderful: look at that wallpaper, those sheets, the lovely curlicues on the bed, Spencer's glasses. I love all the glistening strands of his hair, and Patricia's hair too, perhaps rather unconvincing on her head but her pubic hair is soft and fluffy.

It is an exciting picture visually, with the impressively weird bodily colouring, she a lurid mixture of pinks, yellows and purples, and he two-toned, with the corpse-like lividity of his body and the hectic emotional flush of his face, with its darkly stubbled cheeks. Yet the general impression I receive is vaguely comic: a funny little man with a scraggy neck and his glasses on the end of his nose, gazing vacantly past, not even at, this siren whom he feels is so seductive but who strikes us as so heavily unattractive. She is Patricia Preece, the upper-class girl who tantalized Stanley into marrying her and divorcing his dearly loved Hilda, to whom he carried on writing every day. They had one night together, Patricia having made it a condition that he first sign over to her the deeds of the house; then it was goodbye Stanley, and welcome back live-in girlfriend.

At some level Stanley knows that they can never be united: his art knows it though he himself does not. The very contrasts of their body colours, and her obvious lack of interest, make this clear. She is not spread out for his delectation, she is acting as though he was not there, which, for her, he clearly never was. He looks not at her but into emptiness with a set, bewildered, unhappy expression, yet he insists on painting them as a pair.

I can see that at one level we have something very interesting here, something poignant, a man unable to get through to the woman he loves, and it is not meant to be amusing. Yet it is both funny and sad, and we have to make up our minds as to whether he holds these elements in a unity or whether the picture fragments like the relationship it depicts.

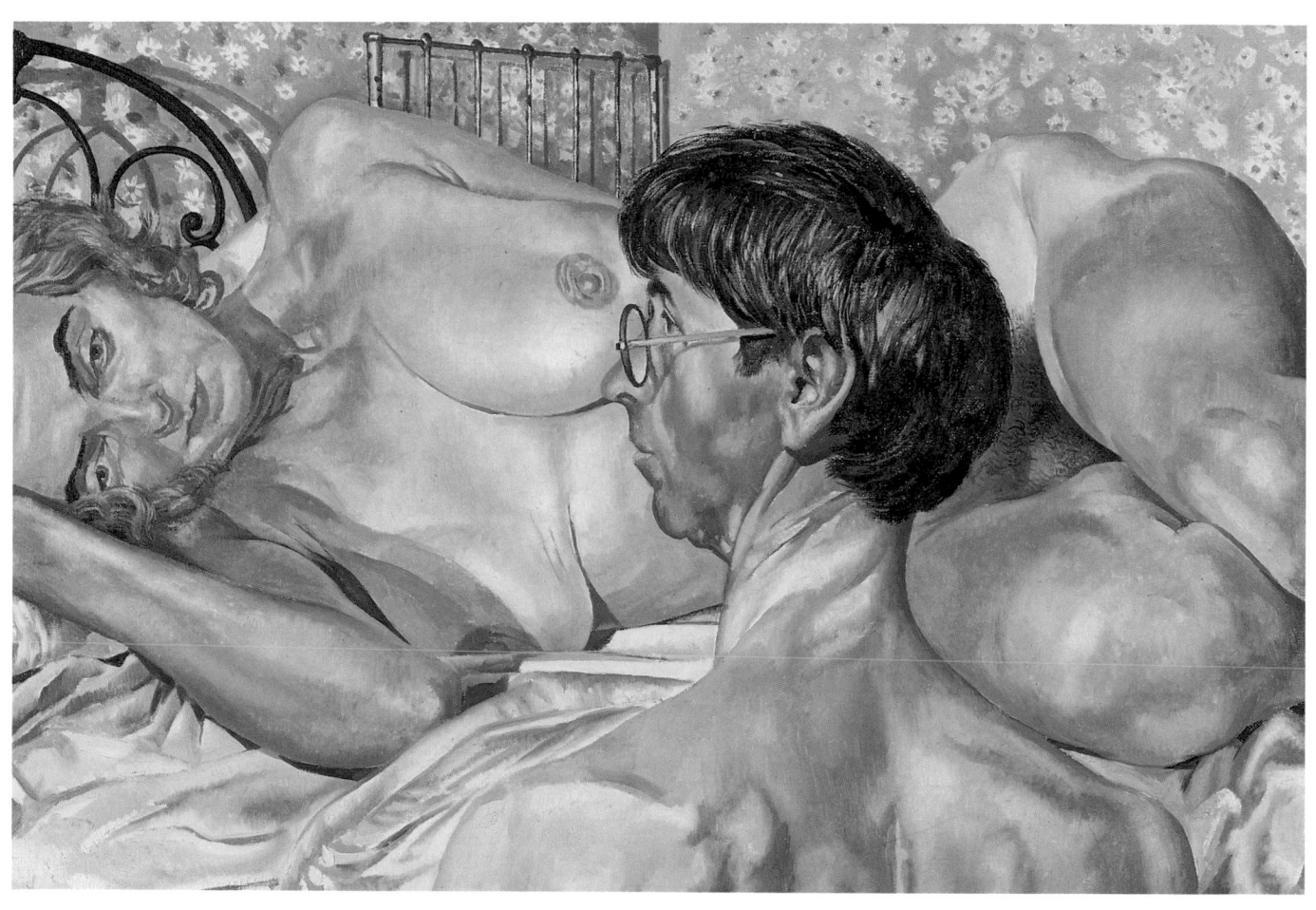

Self-portrait with Patricia Preece **Stanley Spencer** **1936**
Oil on canvas   61 × 91.4cm (24 × 36in)
Fitzwilliam Museum, Cambridge (on loan to Tate Gallery, Liverpool 1992)

Fitzwilliam Museum

CAMBRIDGE

Cambridge was another city that was from the first a certainty for the odyssey, but I had to decide exactly where to go. Many of the colleges have treasures of art, the best known being the richly glowing Rubens *Adoration of the Magi* in King's College Chapel. A recent development has been the acquisition by many college common rooms of some impressive contemporary art. Jesus College has some magnificent works, such as one of Richard Long's stone circles spreading out in a small quadrangle and bringing the world of prehistory into this medieval building. While we were there, this college was having an exhibition of contemporary sculpture, with an unforgettable work, *Learning To Be* by Antony Gormley, planted beneath a huge tree. Gormley makes leaden casts from his own body, and this still figure, tense with desire, clenched fists eager to soar into freedom but held for ever in the earth, planted there like the tree but not by nature, is a superb example of the moral power of great art.

New Hall, a women's college, was also having an exhibition, or rather preparing for one. They had asked contemporary women artists, of the stature of Maggi Hambling and Paula Rego, to donate works to be hung in perpetuity, and it was hard not to stay there and devote the whole programme to these powerful and beautiful works. But, in the end, I felt it had to be the Fitzwilliam Museum, one of the greatest small museums in the world. One of my best-loved Titians is there, there is a grand Veronese (though in the end I felt this picture falls into two fine but separate halves), there are splendid Impressionists, ceramics, bronzes. The collection is almost too rich, and favourite after favourite had to be discarded reluctantly from what could be filmed.

*T*itian was one of those lucky artists, like Rembrandt, whose work became better and better as he grew older. He was well over eighty when he painted this, by special request, for Philip II of Spain.

It is the story of Tarquin and Lucretia, a complicated tale about the abuse of power. Tarquin was the son of the last king of Rome and he felt his rank entitled him to do what he pleased with the Roman women. He approached Lucretia, a chaste Roman wife, and insisted that she sleep with him. When she refused his demands, he threatened to kill her and the poor slave we can just see cowering in the background, and swear he found them sleeping together. He then raped her. In the morning, she called together her family, told them she could not live dishonoured by what had happened, and killed herself.

Everything in this picture shows us what it means for one person to rape another, which is, of course, the ultimate expression of contempt. Notice how their eyes do not meet. She is looking at him, tearfully, pleading. He is not looking at her at all. She does not matter to him: she is a thing, she is for using. (This is the only sin, essentially, to treat somebody or even something with disrespect.)

What is so wonderful about this picture is that at first it seems to show brutal strength triumphing over complete innocence and vulnerability. Titian contrasts them at every point. Her hands are open, reaching out piteously for the help that never comes. His are clenched, grasping things: he is a taker, completely out for self. He is clothed, she is not. He is hard, thrusting, vigorous, destructive. She is soft and defenceless, lying there on piles of white cushions, gleaming out of the darkness of the room. Their legs are parallel, a sign they will never meet; they are set on different courses, the one who wants to destroy and the one who wants to keep her integrity.

Yet, though at first we see greedy power defeating goodness, what Titian actually shows us is the opposite. In his cruelty, his rape of Lucretia, Tarquin destroyed not her, but himself. He so antagonized men of goodwill that they rose in revolt and drove him out of the city. So really it is not so much the rape of Lucretia as the rape of Tarquin. It is she who keeps her integrity, not he. What old Titian is saying, in his wisdom, is that whenever we rape another, which we can do in many ways beside the physical, the real victim, the real ravished one, is ourselves, because we have lost our integrity.

Tarquin and Lucretia **Titian** c.1570
Oil on canvas   182 × 140cm (74⅜ × 57⅛in)
Fitzwilliam Museum, Cambridge

L'Enlèvement (The Abduction)

Paul Cézanne

Born Aix-en-Provence, France 1839
Died Aix-en-Provence, France 1906

~

*I*t is fascinating to compare Titian's treatment of rape, who as an old wise artist could look at it from a great distance, with that of the young Cézanne, to whom it was still a practical, fearful possibility. Strictly speaking, Cézanne's picture is not called the rape but *The Abduction*, and you can see that the dividing line is extremely fine. Here we have a very young man, struggling painfully from his adolescent horrors into maturity. This picture is almost an exorcism.

Cézanne suffered enormously from the turgid, unhealthy, tempting perplexities of a slow-maturing adolescent. They made him wretched. The very thickness of the paint is indicative of an emotional confusion, as he fought to get free from his fixation on dark things: murders, rapes, feuds, misshapen creatures.

One of the ways he has struggled to distance himself here is by setting the event in a sort of pastoral scene. There are two nymphs disporting themselves vaguely in the background, and the abductor's hair is rather longer than was usual in the nineteenth century when this was painted. He may have made it palatable to himself by setting it in another world, but he has not really diffused the erotic energy of it. The dark male has swelling muscles but we cannot see his face and the female looks as if she were dead. She lies there, absolutely limp, frighteningly white, offering no resistance. In theory, this young man could simply be conveying his fainting girlfriend back to her mamma, but when we look at the painting, we know at once that something sinister is afoot.

The landscape echoes this, with gloomy forests encroaching upon the pair, shutting them in. The sky is dark and a mountain blocks the horizon. Everything cries out that these two are trapped, and we feel that the male is just as trapped as the female. All around there is autumnal foliage disintegrating, the atmosphere grows ominous and the dark, rolling paint seems to speak of a dark, rolling imagination. There is a strong note of personal desperation here. Cézanne seems to have led an almost blameless life, but it was one plagued by terrible fears. It is not 'out there' that the action is taking place, but within the painter's own self, and we are moved and even awed, perhaps, by his honesty and his courage.

L'Enlèvement (The Abduction) **Paul Cézanne 1867**

Oil on canvas 90.5 × 117cm (35⅝ × 46in)

Fitzwilliam Museum, Cambridge, by kind permission of the Provost and Fellows of King's College, Cambridge

*S*ince I could only discuss such a few pictures and sculptures, I decided never to do two works by the same artist. But Cézanne is the exception, not because he is my favourite artist (though he is), but because this same room at the Fitzwilliam contained, on another wall, an example of a late Cézanne. This is what makes the early work so infinitely moving. This confused, passionate young man, who could not get his emotions into order but who battled with them so desperately, matured into the most orderly and lucid artist in history. He took his dark, swirling heart and forced it into wisdom and beauty, a transformation that is artistically unique.

This landscape is not an exceptional example of his late work, but is important for its very ordinariness. Cézanne contemplated the world with such intensity and reverence that he could take its full complexity, its essential elusiveness, and turn it into a supremely calm and ordered vision. What he understood is that reality does not stand still for us to outline it. It is continually in a state of flux: at every moment the light changes, every small movement we make affects the view. We can never be detached observers but are of our nature a part of what we see — and what we paint.

The brightness, clearness, beauty of this landscape comes from the artist's humility in its presence. Trees and skies, grass and shadows: all are painted as if from within their own truth, with Cézanne a humble sharer of their world. He never came to the end of his wonder, his overwhelming fascination with the world he lived in. He feared that he spoiled his art because of his own imagined lack of the goodness so radiantly obvious to him in nature, in mountain or still life, in the human body, in material existence. He made no distinction between the matter of earth and the spirit, but he saw them as infusing each other naturally, as they do in humanity. There is not much to get hold of verbally in a great Cézanne. It is too simple, too profound, too beautiful, to be grasped by anything less than love.

Landscape **Paul Cézanne** c.1900
Oil on canvas   62.2 × 51.5cm (24½ × 20¼in)
Fitzwilliam Museum, Cambridge

*T*he Fitzwilliam has three Renoirs and I had intended to speak about none of them. Yet, looking closely at *The Gust of Wind*, I was bowled over by it. Here is a work that completely sums up what Impressionism is and why we love it. In fact, it is because we do all love Impressionist artists that I had decided at first not to include them in the odyssey. I wanted to speak mostly about the less familiar artists, who are too easily overlooked when we go round museums. But this small Renoir painting forced its way past my defences.

It shows quite a simple little hillside, where there is nothing of exceptional quality, no outstanding natural beauty. But over this small hillside a light wind is blowing, and Renoir manages to do what no artist in history had done before: miraculously, he seizes the moment. For ever, now, that breeze will blow. It blows, it moves, and then it dies into stillness. This momentary happening, this small but lovely event, is captured in the paint. This is the effect all the Impressionists wanted to achieve, to give you the feel, the sight, of one moment in time.

Renoir is not one of my favourite artists and I sometimes find his work a little sugary, but in front of this I want to beat my breast and bewail my blindness. How could I have missed what a wonder it is? Here is a magical, glowing evocation of that morning when a young man stood on a hill, watching a faint wind suddenly disturb the grasses, and managed to make it stay there for ever. For ever we can stand there too and watch the grass blowing in the wind. This is to escape time and experience eternity.

This small, unpretentious picture shows us what the spiritual in art is all about. Renoir takes us out of our confines, our ego-cage, into a timeless world, and our stay in it leaves us changed. It would be futile to try to say precisely how we are changed, but great art can be recognized subjectively by the effect it has on us. We have been enlarged in our own being by receiving the blessing of another's.

Le Coup de Vent (The Gust of Wind) **Auguste Renoir** **c.1872–5**
Oil on canvas   52 × 82.5cm (20½ × 32½in)
Fitzwilliam Museum, Cambridge

*P*alma Vecchio has a confusing name. It means 'Palma the Old', but since he died in his late forties it is merely a way of distinguishing him from Palma Giovane, 'Palma the Young'.

This is one of Palma Vecchio's greatest works, both for its splendid visual beauty and the implications of the story it tells. This is the mysterious tale of Venus, Cupid and the arrow. We might think it is nothing more than a delightful depiction of the goddess of love and her child, two beautiful blonde creatures in the Italian sunlight, but actually it is a very subtle contemplation of the responsibility of love. Nobody can quite made out here whether Venus is taking the arrow or giving it. To me, it looks as if she is taking the arrow and trying to make it clear to her small son that if he holds the arrows of love, he must use them responsibly. Cupid has been going round making the wrong people fall in love with each other, and his mother is giving him a stern maternal rebuke: this will not do! That was Cupid's weakness, to be a child who was also a god and to use his powers mischievously.

Here Palma puts before us one of the central human needs, to fall in love with the right person, someone who can respond to you as deeply as you to him or her, bringing you mutual fulfilment. There in the background is the world, with everybody going about their own concerns, wholly unaware that one of the deepest causes of human happiness is being settled here, in this sunlit glade. Will Venus manage to control the little god of love and teach him responsibility? Or will he go on being naughty?

We can see that flowers are springing into existence round her because adult love is fruitful. Behind the mother rises the great solid city: she is mature, her love lasts. Behind the child there is just potential, love that could last but may not. Their faces are very moving: we see grave motherly affection in Venus's concerned expression, and a shamefaced bravado in the little Cupid who knows quite well he has mis-behaved. This is one of those marvellous pictures that succeeds in handling a serious theme with exquisite lightness.

Venus and Cupid **Palma Vecchio** **c.1520–5**
Oil on canvas   118.1 × 208.9cm (46½ × 82⅛in)
Fitzwilliam Museum, Cambridge

Ashmolean Museum

OXFORD

Forty years ago I was just finishing my degree at Oxford. I stayed in the Notre Dame convent on Woodstock Road where we had a new Reverend Mother who was very nervous about young student nuns adrift in the great university. She told me always to remember that the rule of silence applied to my contacts with other students, which meant that conversation must be confined to courtesies and necessities: no idle banter, no long involved philosophical discussions, so dear to the student mind! This gave me a magical Oxford, both part of the life and removed from it. Going straight out to lectures and tutorials meant that I never went into the Ashmolean Museum, though I passed it every day. It may be that I passed by wistfully, but I remember only my brimming happiness at Oxford, my sense of God's presence everywhere, my gratitude to Him for all I was receiving. Dense young woman that I was, it never entered my head that there were areas of myself shut off from God because they were shut off from reality. Both art and literature have helped to unlock these hidden blanks within. Probably, had I gone into the Ashmolean then, it would not have been with the reverent excitement that I went into it on the odyssey. It was an overwhelming joy, to see at last — and at a time when I was ready, or at least less unready, to see them truly — so many of the greatest human creations. Once again, it was a struggle to choose. I would have loved to dwell on a row of small and marvellous Corot landscapes, early works where his infinitely delicate sense of tone is supremely beautiful in its truthfulness. There was a very strong Gerard Terborch, a rider seen from the back, jogging sadly home after a battle, horse and man weary and disheartened. But in the end, the coincidence of the Ashmolean's Filippo Lippi being complemented by the Christ Church Gallery's Filippino Lippi meant that I could look at masterpieces by a father and son both equally illustrious: a rare combination!

*U*ccello's *A Hunt in a Forest* is, I suppose, one of the most famous paintings of the fifteenth century. It seems it is what it says it is: a hunt in a forest. We can have enormous enjoyment watching all these hunters with their various expressions and activities, and the hounds, horses and bounding stags. One man has pulled his horse up and is shrieking aloud to his friends, another is mad with excitement and the hounds seem to crush us forward with their speed.

Yet the fascination of the picture goes deeper than this. It is really a hunt for the passion of Uccello's life, which was perspective. The whole picture is geared to what? To the vanishing point: that is the unseen centre that unifies everything. It is a picture of the most intense concentration on something that is not literally there. The central stag is not there, he is somehow 'beyond', and it is this invisible quarry – not the fleeting stags that we can see, in rather surprising numbers – that unites all the figures we are looking at. The unseen stag is the source of all the excitement: all the dogs frantically running, all the horses moving inexorably into the wood, all the men worked up by the anticipation of the hunt's end.

We could say that the whole scene is about concentration, about homing in on that still centre in our being that we cannot see or get at but that we know exists. Ideally, we would want our whole lives organized, directed toward that vanishing point. I can almost feel a sort of holy envy for Uccello, whose own life was totally fixed on the point that mattered most to him.

In the fifteenth century, perspective was a new discovery. It came as a wonderful mathematical concept that organized what one saw and made order out of the chaos. We are told that Uccello used to sit up all night, sighing over the wonder and pleasure of being able to make sense of his world and crying out: Oh, how beautiful is this perspective! For us the beauty is to see how he made his new understanding visual, showing us how a central point meant that the calm of pattern could be imposed on everything and life given a meaning. It is appropriate that he was called Uccello, which means 'bird', because he shares with us a bird's-eye view, that of a low-flying bird who can see further than the groundlings and who glimpses what they cannot: the unseen stag, the vanishing point, life's still and secret centre.

A Hunt in a Forest **Paolo Uccello** **c.1470**
Tempera with oil on panel   73 × 177cm (28¾ × 69¾in)
Ashmolean Museum, Oxford

*P*iero di Cosimo's *The Forest Fire* is an uncanny picture, painted by a very weird man. Piero was so wholly committed to his art that he lived on boiled eggs, cooking fifty at a time so that he would not have to waste his psychic energy on anything but what truly mattered to him (an attitude with which I feel much sympathy, though not with the egg arrangement). What makes this picture particularly intriguing is that he was terrified of fire, and perhaps what we have here is a man confronting his deepest fears. First we are struck by the eerie sight of the fire, so central and so strangely contained, invoking so many different responses: the birds mostly hysterical, the little family of bears exhausted by their flight, the cowherd with his yoked neck taking only a rather abstract interest in it all. Then we notice that some of the animals have human faces, and we realize that Piero is showing us what he imagines to be a time so far back in the mists of history that the distinction between animal and human had not yet been worked out.

What is at the heart of this picture may be an awareness of the mystery of identity, a puzzlement as to what it really means to be a human being, as opposed to an animal. The animals here have noble human faces, whereas the man has a rather sluggish look.

Clearly Piero sees the animal as potentially a very dignified creature, with a fine and philosophical expression. We have all surely been moved at times by seeing in an animal something purer and better than we see in ourselves.

Where did the fire come from? Was it lightning, nobody's 'fault'? Or was it man, playing with sticks, a mischief-maker from the start, too ignorant to be in control of the world?

Some pictures you can approach beating on a drum and exclaiming repeatedly how wonderful they are: they open themselves to our gaze at once. But others we have to feather into opening up, allowing their magic to steal over us gradually. This painting is so extraordinary, such a haunting vision of a world that never was and yet exists so poetically in the mind of the artist. He is trying to tell us something that he himself cannot express, and I am afraid that I can do no more than point to it.

Fra Filippo Lippi

Born Florence, Italy 1406
Died Spoleto, Italy 1469

~

*T*his is a picture of great poignancy, almost a heart-rending picture, not just because of the work itself — so small, delicate and beautiful — but because of the story of the artist who painted it. He is known as Fra Filippo Lippi, and 'Fra' is a rough equivalent of our 'Reverend': he was a monk. He had been abandoned on the streets of Florence and the monks took him in, which in those days, when vocation was seen differently from the way it is today, meant that he automatically joined the ranks of the brethren.

But Filippo had no desire to be a monk, which is a way of life that only works if you are passionately committed to it (and then it works marvellously). What Filippo needed was the support of a loving partner, someone to cherish and be cherished by, someone to bear him a child, perhaps. As the years went by, and he found himself in and out of trouble, he must have felt that his life would be lonely and barren to the end. Then, at last, he met and fell in love with a nun, the same kind of nun as he was a monk, someone who had not chosen the life freely. They both got dispensations and married, and the child of this union was also a painter, the great Filippino Lippi, little Philip.

Joachim and Anna were the names early legend gave to the parents of the Virgin Mary and the story told how they were childless until their old age. To be barren was then considered to be a sign of divine displeasure and Joachim, a devout priest, and his saintly wife grieved over their mysterious failure. Then, legend has it, he was inspired to go out into the desert where he had a vision that their marriage would be fruitful at last, and Lippi has painted the moment where they met, at the Golden Gate of Jerusalem. From that embrace, miraculously, was said to come the Virgin.

The two elderly people look into each other's eyes with such profound trust, such reverence, such love. All around are animal pairs: nature is fertile. Joachim is coming out of the desert wastes, all stone and emptiness, into the rich fruitful land of love. Unseen hands bless him and his wife: are they those of their grandson-to-be, the Infant Jesus, or of their coming daughter, Mary? Is it she who stands behind them, or an angel? The emotion is overwhelming here: the glad, tremulous, deeply-felt gratitude of a lonely misfit in life who has at last glimpsed the vision of human happiness and fulfilment.

The Forest Fire **Piero di Cosimo**   c.1505
Tempera on panel 71 × 203cm (28 × 79⅞in)
Ashmolean Museum, Oxford

The Meeting of Joachim and Anna at the Golden Gate   **Fra Filippo Lippi   c.1450–60**
Tempera on panel 20×48cm ($7\frac{7}{8} \times 17\frac{7}{8}$in)
Ashmolean Museum, Oxford

Filippo Lippi died when his son Filippino was about ten and it was Botticelli, a family friend, who trained the boy as an artist. *The Wounded Centaur* has just that lyrical, delicate, moving touch distinguishing his father's work, though this is even more ethereal.

The Greeks thought the centaur — half man, half horse — was a nobler creature than mere man, horses being higher on the moral scale than we are. The very noblest of the centaurs was Chiron, and his story is connected with an arrow. Cupid is here asleep, and Chiron has picked up the arrows of love and wounded himself, a subtle way of hinting that he is playing with temptation. The picture makes it quite clear that he is married: tucked away inside the rock is a little family and he has no right at all to be playing with the idea of infidelity. At this level, the picture is a charming lesson in morality, yet this does not wholly explain the impact it makes on us. Somehow it stirs the heart and we feel that the theme is one that matters to the artist himself.

What we have to remember is that any pupil of Botticelli was well versed in Greek legends, and the myth about Chiron said that he would be killed by a poisoned arrow in the heat of battle. Right at the front of the scene is a frail and broken branch, reminding us that this noble creature is mortal and he too will be broken. It was a sad and treacherous death, yet it was not the true end, since the gods carried him away to the heavens and named him after the constellation Sagittarius, the Archer. He is already a superhuman creature, able to cherish his family in that inhospitable cave in the rock, and he can see what we humans cannot: the reality of Cupid's arrows. So the painting makes gentle play with arrows and fidelity, with temptation and death. But here death is prefigured as overcome; the centaur holding the arrow is reminding us not that those who are curious about love's arrows may get wounded by them, but also that after his death he will become immortal, as a glory of the night skies.

The Wounded Centaur **Filippino Lippi** **c.1500**
Oil on wood 77.5 × 68.5cm (30½ × 27in)
Christ Church Picture Gallery, Oxford

*E*verything Claude painted depicts Arcadia, that distant and golden world of peace. This large painting is one of his very greatest, paradoxically because it tells the haunting story of how Arcadia was lost, a complicated historical legend of how the Trojans were welcomed into Italy until Ascanius betrayed the hospitality they were offered. He shot the sacred stag, and Claude shows us that dramatic moment of tense confrontation in which animal looks at man and man looks back at animal. Ascanius has only to use his mind to know that this is a sacred stag, consecrated to Sylvia, but he refuses to acknowledge this. He is selfishly intent on doing what he loves, which is destroying. Which of us can say: Not me?

What makes this picture so awesome is that his act was not an isolated, inconsequential event: when he shot the sacred stag, civil war broke out. So this shows the very last moment in which the country is at peace. We can see that the stag simply cannot believe that man would be so foolish as to destroy his own happiness, something which has terrible twentieth-century relevance. The world – still bathed in sylvan tranquillity – is darkening towards the evening, with a blue sunset brightness in the sky. We see a great ruined temple, a sad suggestion of what is soon to come. The trees are leaning forward as if to grieve and there is no visible sun, just twilight and a sense of the world holding its breath. There are empty boats, people fleeing, but nothing has actually happened yet. All waits at that moment when Ascanius can still choose. Will he shoot the arrow or will he not? (And will we too shoot the arrow? Will we destroy our planet or will we hold back in time?)

What gives this painting its extra edge is that this was the last work Claude ever painted. In a way, his own life is the stag, with the arrow pointed at it, and he waits incredulously for death. But on a deeper level, this is his last legacy to us: the knowledge that there *is* an Arcadia, a world of peace and sunlight where everything is quiet and blessed, but if we want to, we can destroy it, as Ascanius is poised to do.

Landscape with Ascanius Shooting the Stag of Sylvia **Claude Lorrain 1682**
Oil on canvas   120 × 150cm (47⅛ × 59in)
Ashmolean Museum, Oxford

Wilton House

Wilton House
SALISBURY

Some of the finest art in Britain is in stately homes. In a small panelled room under the stairs at Drumlanrig Castle, the Duke of Buccleuch has a Holbein, a perhaps-Leonardo and one of the greatest Rembrandts in the world. Anglesey Abbey has two magnificent Claudes, Burghley House has a *Madonna and Child* by Orazio Gentileschi with a most striking saffron robe for the Virgin and a Veronese altarpiece in the private chapel. The special glory of Wilton House is that it is the birthplace of great literature as well as great art. Sir Philip Sidney wrote *Arcadia* there, while staying with his sister, and it is said that the first production of Shakespeare's *Twelfth Night* was at Wilton.

Walking across the lawns to the river, looking up to the gentle hill behind on which a former Earl of Pembroke built a Grecian temple, standing on the gracious Palladian bridge amidst the silence, it is easy to believe that this is place of creative blessedness. It was originally a convent and a great sense of happiness still pervades the house and grounds. Whatever human sorrow and error has taken place there, and the Pembrokes were no more immune than any other family, the dominant note is of peace.

It is an absolute treasure-house of art. The most famous rooms – the Double Cube and the Single Cube – were specially built for an artistic purpose by Inigo Jones, but the most remarkable room is the small corner chamber which is nothing less than a giant jewel-box. Masterpieces line every wall, pour out from over doors, bedeck the chimneypiece. One feels dazzled and dazed: it was very hard to pick and choose when on every side there were works vying for attention and admiration. If I had been entirely alone and free, I would not have included van Dyck in my odyssey, but Wilton is the home of the largest and greatest van Dycks ever painted, commissioned by the fourth Earl, who was an early patron of the artist. Nobody could go to Wilton without talking about the van Dycks, and moreover, talking about them with pleasure and a sense of fresh discovery.

The fourth Earl of Pembroke built a special room, a great double cube, thirty by sixty (9.15 by 18.3 metres), in honour of the huge painting he commissioned from his friend, van Dyck, as a family portrait. Yet it is more than just a family portrait, because the Earl had several goals he wanted to achieve in one grandiloquent swoop. First, of course, he wanted to show off his family. Next to him is his second wife, looking rather dour (she is mother to none of these children). Beside her is his only daughter, Sophia, with her husband, and on the other side there are five of his sons, with the three who have died shown above as cherubs.

This is also a wedding portrait and, if we look closely, we can see that the centre of the picture is not really the Earl but the young bride, Mary Villiers, a slender figure in ivory satin with silver lace. She was a great prize, the beloved ward of Charles I, and the family who won her was receiving a signal honour. This picture trumpets aloud to the great families of England the King's special favour. The bridegroom behind her, the heir, is sixteen and she is thirteen. We may not be able to guess that from their faces, but one can never tell very much from any of van Dyck's faces: he was a supreme flatterer. There must have been a certain likeness, but by and large he was a society painter who made everybody look grandly aristocratic, glittering in their silks and velvets.

Usually, this kind of cosmetic art is not all that interesting, yet this is an enthralling work and we may wonder why. I think it is because there is a kind of subtext. The young man right at the edge of the group — Sophia's husband, Lord Caernarvon — is going to be killed soon in the coming Civil War. The beautiful arrogant young bridegroom in his ruffled silks will be dead a few months later from smallpox and Mary Villiers will marry again and pass out of the family. Obviously, van Dyck could not have known this, but he may have been aware, at some level, that England was heading for a dreadful war, and that the glittering youth he painted were soon to die in battle.

One can spend time before this picture wondering what these people were really like. The Earl and his dark gloomy Countess: did they love each other? And the young couples, whose lives together were to be so short: how happy were they? Does it mean anything that everyone is looking in a different direction: were they united or apart? On the surface all looks so glamorous and romantic, but what was the truth? We can never know.

Philip, 4th Earl of Pembroke and his Family **Sir Anthony van Dyck** **1634/5**
Oil on canvas   335.3 × 518.2cm (132 × 204in)
Wilton House, Salisbury

*V*an Dyck's great gift was to show the exterior of a person in all its splendour and beauty; what does not interest him is the human heart. Rembrandt took a totally different approach: he was interested in the true self, the inner truth, and he only values appearances for what they could reveal of that interior. Looking at this portrait, labelled 'Rembrandt', we can see it immediately. This demonstrates how labels can sometimes assume too much importance, because scholars now agree that it is actually not by Rembrandt at all, but by his friend, Jan Lievens. They shared a studio and must have used the same old woman, who may or may not be the mother of one of them, as a model. When we look 'through' the label, we see only what the label suggests. Say 'Rembrandt', and we see at once the inner self: the old woman's complete absorption in her book, and the moving dignity of old age. When we change the label and say 'Lievens', we may see something quite different, a rather charming but almost comic old lady with her glasses on the tip of her nose, and our attitude towards the painting may change.

This is dangerous. It means we have not seen at all for ourselves but only under the influence of preconceived opinions. We all do it: see the label and read the picture appropriately. Unconsciously we are playing safe, not trusting our own response but hiding behind accepted judgements. (This is the great value of contemporary art, that it forces us to look without protection and take the risk of making fools of ourselves.)

Here, in the *Portrait of the Artist's Mother*, we have a perfect opportunity to disregard reputation and simply look at the painting. What do we see? If we insist it is by Rembrandt we may see 'too much', and if we admit it is by Lievens we may see 'too little'! Seeing for ourselves, just as it is, we may be able to recognize that this is a wonderful picture, strong and sensitive and sharply perceptive of old age. We can look at it and delight in it and be warmed at heart by it. We can forget all about the labels.

Portrait of the Artist's Mother **Jan Lievens** **1629**
Oil on canvas   75.6 × 63.5cm (29¾ × 25in)
Wilton House, Salisbury

A Piper

Giovanni Savoldo

Born Brescia, Italy c.1480
Died Venice(?), Italy c.1550

~

Prince Rupert of the Rhine

Gerrit van Honthorst

Born Utrecht, the Netherlands 1590
Died The Hague, the Netherlands 1656

~

St Anthony the Hermit

Lorenzo Lotto

Born Venice(?), Italy c.1480
Died Loreto, Italy 1556

~

These three portraits are impressive in themselves but perhaps even more so when compared with each other. Savoldo's *Piper* has a mystical haunting quality that makes it unforgettable. He holds a pipe and looks out at us with a grave and vulnerable beauty. He is a youth in his full springtime glory, and yet the face seems so aware that he and all of us will have to die. The pipe is a sort of frozen music, recalling Keats's lines about piping 'to the spirit Ditties of no tone'. The boy looks out in this context of silent music, seeming to question us as we pass by.

When we do pass by, we come to another and perhaps equally beautiful picture of a young man. Nobody knows who the piper was, merely a youth who caught Savoldo's eye with his dreamy, apprehensive beauty. But Honthorst's young man is Prince Rupert of the Rhine, the great hero of the Civil War. He came to England to be the leader of his royal uncle's cavalry, and here he is in all the majesty of noble youth, with his long serious aristocratic face. He took his life into his hands again and again, and it was highly likely that he would meet his death in a reckless cavalry charge. It is a contradictory face, with its girlish ringlets and powerful, almost arrogant expression: a portrait of a young hero. Yet it is not a poetic face: Savoldo's boy was the poetry, facing into a shadowy future, holding on to his pipe as if music is going to be his guide to the complexities and dangers ahead. Rupert ignores the dangers: his is an epic face: resolute, pale and absurdly brave.

Nothing could be less like the marvellous Lotto *St Anthony*. I particularly like Lotto, a devious off-beat artist always, who is here pretending that someone called Anthony is the saintly hermit of legend. He looks at us with complacent solemnity, apparently unaware that Lotto has fitted him out with a large and elaborately laundered white collar, which would be hard to come by in the Egyptian desert. St Anthony was famous for his temptations, and we can see a whiskered monster clambering out of hell towards the saint, who is blissfully unconcerned, pointing airily out towards the world while demons rage at his feet. The artist is giving us a strong nudge in the ribs, and this secret chuckle makes it one of the most delightful of pictures. Lotto never wants us to take him entirely seriously, but that is his greatness. He makes us smile at the wonder of life and its mystery.

A Piper **Giovanni Savoldo**
DATE UNKNOWN
Oil on canvas   52 × 40.6cm (20½ × 16in)
Wilton House, Salisbury

Prince Rupert of the Rhine
Gerrit van Honthorst   1636
Oil on wood   76.2 × 59.7cm (30 × 23½in)
Wilton House, Salisbury

St Anthony the Hermit **Lorenzo Lotto** DATE UNKNOWN
Oil on wood   34.3 × 40cm (13½ × 15¾in)
Wilton House, Salisbury

This painting, though not large, has enormous emotional impact. Think of how they queue up in the Louvre to look at *Mona Lisa*, and though this is not by Leonardo but by his pupil, da Sesto, he is using a Leonardo drawing and copying one of his lost masterpieces. It is a peculiarly moving picture of a woman being loved by something non-human. The swan, of course, is Jove, who was forever falling in love with nymphs and girls, pursuing them and being repulsed until he got through their chaste defences, by disguise.

Here he has transformed himself into a swan, but it is a very tender image. He is a big and loving swan, with his wings around Leda, enfolding her, stretching his great beak up to her ear to give her a little love nibble. She is looking down, proud and shy at her lover's embrace. But I think there is a note of sadness here too, in her Mona Lisa smile and downward look. If your lover is a swan there cannot be very much communication in the relationship. It is a doomed love, and her wistful look suggests that she is already aware of that.

Yet this is not a sad picture. We are seeing a moment of joy and pride, as the parents see their children being born: half his, hence the eggs; half hers, hence the babies. I have heard, with astonishment, a historian lament the pain this birth must have cost her, but one glance at that firm and supple young body tells us that the eggs are not meant to be taken literally. They are part of the myth, a poetic fancy meant to show that you will not have normal children if you fall in love with a swan. It will mean loneliness, and a certain generic distancing from your children, yet you will be swept up into a magic and mysterious atmosphere.

Even at one remove, the Leonardesque enchantment is at work, opening up a great misty background of mountain ranges, suggesting infinite possibilities. Flowers spring up at her feet, and her hair waves in floating tendrils around her lovely face. This is a glorious depiction of love, of sadness, of the mingled joy and pain of becoming a parent, and of the mythical world that we can never enter literally but to which works like this give us access.

Leda and the Swan   **Cesare da Sesto**   1506–10
Oil on wood   96.5 × 73.7cm (38 × 29in)
Wilton House, Salisbury

I have a humiliating confession to make about this painting. I knew that there was a picture at Wilton of the Athenian philosopher Democritus by the great Spanish painter Jusepe de Ribera and I was very eager to see it. I came bounding into the house, looked at the picture and walked on, unimpressed. As I moved around on the hunt for more glamorous paintings, I began to have a strange sense of having been put to a test, a moral test, and that I had failed it. I felt so uneasy that, almost to reassure myself, I came back and looked again. This time I stood rooted to the spot, overwhelmed, because this is indeed an overwhelming picture. It is one of enormous integrity, a very quiet slow work, with nothing about it to seduce the frivolous. Mea culpa! I had not been intent enough to see the great strength and purity here, the absolute lack of self-dramatization both by the artist and of the subject.

Democritus was famous for being the laughing philosopher, which does not mean that he was one of those resolutely cheerful people who make light of all life's difficulties. Rather, it means he was one of those strong people who can see life in its true perspective. They say that he smiled at the follies of mankind, but not cynically. He too was part of mankind, and he felt we are all of us foolish, not least himself.

This is a wonderful portrait of a strong, brave man. He is very poor. We see the poor quality of his clothes, the holes in them, his garments roughly fumbled together with complete disregard for how he looks. His great treasure is his book: he is a scholar. He looks out with that frank sweetness of one who does not have to fear what others think of him or what the world can do to him. He is contained in his own integrity, his absence of egotism, his unaffected interest in what he sees, hears and knows. It is not a handsome face but a deeply impressive one.

It took me some time before I appreciated the truth and power of this painting. Looking at art can be a daunting business: we uncover things in ourselves that we may not have wanted to know, but we also uncover the freedom of knowing the truth and wanting to become more worthy of it.

Democritus **Jusepe de Ribera** c.1635–7
Oil on canvas   155 × 119.4cm (61 × 47in)
Wilton House, Salisbury

Barber Institute of Fine Arts

BIRMINGHAM

rchitecturally, the city of Birmingham alarmed me. It was an alien landscape, hostile to humans unless armoured in moving vehicles. In happy contrast, in no other place on the odyssey did we receive such a welcome from the director and curators (though Edinburgh, too, gave us a pleasant sense of being seen as creative colleagues). So although as a city I liked Birmingham the least of all those I saw, in terms of the actual galleries my fondest memories are of the Barber Institute there.

We could also have gone to the Birmingham City Art Gallery, a very rich collection, where there is perhaps the finest cluster of the great Pre-Raphaelites, and it is nobody's fault but my own that I do not much care for them. If any work could have lured me to the City Art Gallery, it would have been the tiny painting by Petrus Christus, *The Man of Sorrows*, but it affected me so deeply that I would have found it almost impossible to wax as eloquent as such a masterpiece deserves. We went, then, to the Barber Institute which is part of the University and whose director, Richard Verdi, is a professor there and his head curator, Paul Spencer-Longhurst, is a lecturer.

I am sure that the staff of every museum and stately home have a deep knowledge and love of their collection, alert to all is strengths, active to remedy any weaknesses, continually seeking to enter more sensitively into the form and meaning of every work. But it was above all at the Barber that I actually saw this in action. When I heard that one of the pictures considered 'top' was a Murillo, *The Marriage Feast at Cana*, I realized that I had not looked at it properly, having a foolish prejudice against Murillo. On the other hand, it was an immense inner comfort to know that what had most intrigued my eye was also of outstanding importance to these scholars. Like all true scholars, they never made me feel inadequate, even though by their standards, I most surely am so. Of all the galleries, this is the one I would most like to revisit, even more than my beloved Oxford and my childhood Edinburgh.

By unfortunate accident, the odyssey has an imbalance: there is only one work by a woman artist, which is this fine portrait by Elisabeth Vigée-Lebrun. However it is a splendid work by this painter, who can at times be rather superficial, and it has a special interest for me in that it goes counter to one of my most entrenched convictions. I have long held — and still hold — the certainty that gender is unimportant in art. (It is existentially important, in that women are ignored and their artistic confidence undervalued, but not essentially so.) It is impossible to tell from a work of art whether it was painted or sculpted by a man or a woman. This present work is the only one I have found that seems to me an exception, and even here I cannot tell how much I am influenced by knowing in advance the artist's name.

Vigée-Lebrun clearly liked Vivara Golovine, as we know from her autobiography. She describes her as 'a charming woman, full of wit and talent', very much the sort of compliment that Lebrun would have sought for herself. One cannot help seeing Lebrun as rather a complacent young woman. She was recognized to be both charming and pretty, and certainly her self-portraits show her as such. She tended to flirt through life, making friendships above her station, as with Marie Antoinette. After the French Revolution she skipped off to other European capitals, and here we have her painting the aristocracy in Russia, successful as ever.

One gets the immediate impression that artist and subject have a certain rapport: both sparkle with intelligence and social wit. It is a very beautiful and even erotic portrait, with the great mane of dark curls and bandeau worn so dashingly, the big luminous eyes, the way she has flung up her cape to hold it coquettishly against her cheek. All this any male could have seen, but what this female artist has also brought out is another quality which you can look at and judge for yourself. It is an almost boyish directness, a masculine vigour and power which comes across with enormous assurance. Lebrun is not daunted by the Countess as a certain sort of man might be.

What I find so riveting is that this portrait is an expression of the classic African belief that each of us is really born a twin, and our invisible twin is of the other sex. Here Lebrun shows us both twins, the physical one and the spiritual one that animates it. The beautiful Countess has, mysteriously, the dominance and authority of her male twin-in-heaven, and Lebrun reveals this masculine-femininity.

Countess Golovine **Elisabeth Vigée-Lebrun** c.1797–1800
Oil on canvas 83 × 67cm (32¾ × 26⅜in)
Barber Institute of Fine Arts, Birmingham

*I*n contrast to the Vigée-Lebrun, a woman painted by a woman, Beccafumi shows us a woman painted by a man. This is, of course, a cliché in art, since male artists have had nearly all the opportunities. This *Reclining Nymph* (or Venus, nobody can quite decide) appears to be a further example of a cliché, with all that female flesh exposed to the male view. But we should look again, more closely, since what we have here is actually a very subtle variation on that well-worn theme.

Look at this nymph and her hefty, muscular shoulders, at her arms swelling with power, her great strong legs and that thick and bullish neck. She certainly has a bosom, but it is a minuscule bosom, as if the artist has simply filled out what looks like male flesh to make it a little more rounded. She is not without female curves in parts, but there are more parts that are unambiguously male. Yet on top of this is a ravishing woman's face, with a wistful smile and that delicate little glitter of diamond earring. Her hands are clearly feminine too, with their long, elegant fingers.

Beccafumi makes a deliberately sexist comment by clothing her in a diaphanous gown of changing colours, and underlines this by providing the little Cupid with a windmill: woman is changeable and as variable as the wind. The interesting question is why he has chosen to do this, to make his point and then undermine it by not painting a normal woman's body. It is as if he could not come to terms with womanhood. The actuality of woman seems to daunt him, so that he is forced by his insecurity to make her body into some kind of abstraction, which he can then distance himself from. He puts her in these shimmering acidic colours, gives her an exquisite face and then, duty done, he backs away.

It is precisely this hint of psychological perplexity that makes the picture interesting. Perhaps not everybody will share my delight in it. To me, it is suffused with an air of poetic mystery, painted with immense sensitivity to colour, and I especially love the beautiful anomalous head. But even those who dislike the picture may find it interesting: a woman painted by a man who, like Michelangelo and Leonardo, was wary of women.

Reclining Nymph **Domenico Beccafumi** **c.1519**
Oil on wood 71.7 × 138cm (28¼ × 54¼in)
Barber Institute of Fine Arts, Birmingham

Jan Gossaert tended to call himself 'Mabuse' because he came from the town of Maubeuge and he thought his new name was more elegant. He may have had a problem about his name but he had no problem about relationships and equality. Both partners are treated here with equal dignity and respect, and they treat each other with the same dignified respect. They look at each other with equal affection and tenderness. Hercules is an enormously strong man, but we notice that his massive iron-banded club has been grounded here. Why? Because you do not need a weapon when you are in the presence of one who loves you: there is nothing to defend yourself against. Deianeira has taken off her silken garment with its golden embroidery. Why? Because you do not need the protection of glamorous clothes when you are with one who loves you: you are protected by their love.

They hold each other firmly but non-possessively. As well as holding, they are also leaving each other space. There is a lovely intertwining at the base which represents their unity, and a calm spaciousness above which shows that each allows the other to be their own person. This is the marriage ideal: two people loving, supporting and helping each other to be what each was made to be. They do not try to change each other: they accept, they love, and they confirm.

There is an added dimension to this picture if you know the whole story. As a young woman, Deianeira was almost raped and Hercules, the great warrior, came to her rescue. As the rapist was dying, he whispered to Deianeira that she should dip a cloak in blood and if ever her husband needed help, send it to him. Although she has a face of great sweetness, she does not look like one of the world's great intellects. She believed her attacker, and when Hercules was wounded, wrapped him in the cloak, which was of course poisoned and he died, whereupon the heart-broken Deianira died too.

Something of that human tragedy is hinted at here. The enclosing walls have a tomb-like effect and the pair look as if they are sitting on a sarcophagus. Mabuse may be reminding us that we love until death parts us, and that certain blessed lovers are never parted by death because they die together.

Hercules and Deianeira **Jan Gossaert (Mabuse)** **1517**
Oil on wood   37 × 27cm (14½ × 10⅝in)
Barber Institute of Fine Arts, Birmingham

*R*ubens was one of the most fortunate of people: he was handsome, he was clever, he came of a good family, he was supremely gifted as an artist and seen to be so, everybody liked him, he was always successful and he was a man of transparent goodness. To crown it all, he had a blissful marriage and, when his first wife died and he married again, he had equal success with the second. It has always seemed to me that this picture, which is obviously nothing to do with either of his wives, is nevertheless a wonderful image of a contented marriage.

As he grew older and wealthier, Rubens decided to buy a country estate, Het Steen. He lived there with his second wife and this painting shows his own land. It is as if he is looking out at it and claiming it for himself, taking possession by the transforming action of painting. This was the place where he had made a home for his family, where they lived in happiness together. Yet we can see that this landscape does not sparkle like an Impressionist landscape does. It is not a particularly bright picture, darkened by the rolling cloud that suggests that there is sadness in every life. Even for Rubens, uniquely fortunate as he was, there was the death of his first wife and the affliction of painful gout in his later years.

The darkening skies shadow the land beneath, but it remains beautifully fertile, bathed in a sense of peace and contentment. Interestingly, there is no one in it except one distant peasant, as if Rubens is making a symbolic statement, telling us that it is really he who is in the picture, and the land is himself, not merely his individual self but an extended self, one with his beloved wife and one with the children. He is making visible the place where they flourish: happy people in a happy land.

Rubens had the gift of happiness, not for himself but to share with us, so that it becomes ours too. Looking at a great Rubens can truly give one the experience, even if vicariously, of happiness.

Landscape in Flanders **Sir Peter Paul Rubens** **c.1636**
Oil on wood   90 × 134cm (35½ × 52⅜in)
Barber Institute of Fine Arts, Birmingham

This is a still life by Jan de Heem, one of the very great Dutch still-life painters of the seventeenth century. It is an early work, and he has managed to combine into one dazzling picture two different still-life traditions. He shows us all the opulence and wonder of these massive goblets and plates: they represent art, that which is grand and magnificent and ever-lasting. Yet he also has in the fruit and nuts all the humble rotundities and obliquities and imperfections of nature, which remind us that life is passing. Everything here that is natural will die, is already dying. Everything that is made by the craftsman will survive. He looks at both of them, and he shows them in the same richly glowing colours.

This kind of visual splendour makes one ponder why we find still life so enthralling. It is not because this is just a superb piece of realism, because it is actually fictitious. It is meant to represent a breakfast table, but no ordinary breakfast would ever include in its setting the great nautilus cup, clearly the family pride and joy, nor the other rich tableware. It is a form

of showing off, pretending to be so wealthy that these rare treasures are casually used for the least elaborate meal of the day.

If it is not realism, is it the sensation that we are looking in and sharing in a world that is now gone for ever? This too is not the answer, since we are also fascinated by contemporary still lives. Can it be that what moves us is the reverence which the artist feels, his creative awe at the sight of the beautiful things human beings have made and for the humble things that human beings have taken from the earth? Both have been gained by care and labour. The nautilus cup gleams as a solemn reminder of the sea that shaped it, and the peeled lemon, the bulbous pear, the nuts that have been cracked open and will soon wither, speak of the earth.

There is a dark tonality that gives perfect visual expression to de Heem's awareness of moving out of his own transitoriness into the still, hieratic beauty of a composition that will last eternally and that gives us an understanding of values more enduring than those of the passing days.

Still Life with a Nautilus Cup **Jan Davidsz de Heem 1632**
Oil on wood   78 × 73cm (30¾ × 28¾in)
Barber Institute of Fine Arts, Birmingham

National Gallery of Scotland

EDINBURGH

An odyssey is all about home-coming, and visiting Edinburgh had for me a sense of coming home. I was not born there but in South Africa; my father had a late vocation to medicine and we arrived at the University when I was a very small child. My first memory is of daisies, white against the green of the Meadows, where my mother would push my pram. It must have been a lonely time for my mother and a strenuous time for my father, but I have only radiant recollections. I wish now that we had spent some time in the great Scottish art galleries, where, even for children, there is so much to see and be enriched by. Still, there was a singular thrill in finally seeing Old Masters that I had pored over so often in reproduction. (And not only Old Masters: Peter Randell-Page, the sculptor, had an exhibition at the Royal Botanic Garden when I was there: great, swelling mysterious shapes. Many were out of doors, and despite ubiquitous notices urging nobody to touch them, they were an irresistible magnet for small children, who played with them and on them: a lovely way to get to know an artist's work!)

What I longed above all to see in the National Gallery of Scotland were their two late Titians, and it was a struggle to keep to my self-imposed rule not to repeat any artist. Both paintings are sublimely poetical musings about myths of Diana, the virgin goddess, and the inexorability of divine law.

Sir Timothy Clifford took time from a crowded schedule to show us the preparations for their forthcoming exhibition of Dutch art in Scotland, which was a joy and privilege, not just because of the art but because of his educated enthusiasm. The same was true at the Scottish National Portrait Gallery, where I listened to Duncan Thomson and his chief curator and learned from their love of their collection. The most blissful encounter of all was in the upper room at the National Gallery, where they have a magnificent collection of late medieval works, with some majestic Raphaels among them, aloofly marking the gap between the relatively unsophisticated world of minor artists and the lofty splendour of genius. In this context Raphael looked almost too perfect, too fearsomely gifted. It is always the small and wonderful medieval artists who overpower me with the excitement of living in a world where such things exist.

*B*ypassing the great Raphael, I was captivated by this *Madonna and Child* by a completely unknown painter from the Italian town of Ferrara. It was a small town and we might say that he is a small artist, but so he thinks himself. He has made no attempt to emulate the sublimities of the great but has simply stayed within his own limitations and made the very best of them.

It is a charming picture. To begin with, he has very wittily set the whole thing in a false frame. It is as if the panel had been wrapped in paper, and he has pulled it off, leaving jagged scraps round the edges, surrounding the 'wooden' frame inside. On one of the scraps of paper a convincing fly has settled. Art historians seized eagerly upon this and deduced that he must be revealing his name: Mosca, the Italian for fly. They then discovered to their consternation that there was no artist of this name in Ferrara at the time, so we are left with the fact that we shall never know the identity of this man with his enchanting wit and vision.

We peer past the frames as if through a window, to see the Virgin sitting on a deliciously pink aqueduct. She is a huge figure, she fills the sky, but through the arches we can catch enticing glimpses of Ferrara, little visions of the world of earth. Tripping on at either side are two more denizens of heaven, absolutely delightful angels, with dancing feet shod in neat scarlet slippers. Their wings are like bright spires, narrow streaks of feathered gaiety, far too slight to bear their body weight. They are not meant to be real wings, merely to sketch for us the idea of wing, the idea of angel.

The Christ child is a real child, not a miniature emperor; he is wailing and tugging at his mother's clothes to get her to take notice, while she is wholly oblivious, looking away into the distance, gently suggesting the idea of the Virgin in majesty, and holding in her hand a pomegranate. This is a symbol of Resurrection, rebirth, and although the picture is so light, so playful, it is still a very serious painting. It belongs to the world of the Resurrection, where all is joy and weightlessness. The artist is sharing with us the wonder of knowing that ours is not the only world in existence. There is another, the home of Virgin and Child and light-footed angels, a world that diminishes huge bridges and tears away the paper anxieties of the earth below. I am almost glad he enjoys the selflessness of anonymity.

Madonna and Child with Two Angels **Unknown Ferrarese artist   15th century**
Oil on wood   58.4 × 44.1cm (23 × 17⅜in)
National Gallery of Scotland, Edinburgh

*I*t is impossible not to feel that Gerard David has a twinkle in his eye — a reverent twinkle, of course — as he sets out three of the stories legendarily told of St Nicholas. No sooner was the saint born than he is said to have stood erect and praised God, adding that in a spirit of self-denial he would refrain from his mother's breast three times a week. David shows us the exhausted astonishment of his mother, while the midwife bathing him turns to her in humorous consternation.

A child so set upon sanctity was a natural candidate for the church, and we see him next in the role of benevolent pastor. An impoverished nobleman is grimly contemplating the fate of his three motherless and, more to the point, dowerless daughters. They lie on the right, three to a bed, placid little faces propped up on their pillow, while their anxious father keeps vigil. St Nicholas is about to drop three golden balls on to the floor, an anonymous dowry for the daughters. (It was imaginative acts of generosity like this that later transformed him into Santa Claus. The three golden balls live on in a more dubious context, too, as the symbol of pawnbrokers.)

The last picture sees him a bishop and a still more astonishing worker of wonders. It is a time of famine and three small boys have mysteriously disappeared, while a certain merchant is offering for sale a large vat of salted pork. Wise in the ways of the wicked world, the saint makes a sign of the cross over the brine-tub, and out step the three missing children, who have been cut up and salted. The saint's prayer reintegrates them, still looking rather bewildered by their experience, and brings them back to the world where they belong.

At one level, these are charming anecdotes, told with graphic skill and glorious brightness of colour. But they are more than that. David is making three moral points, gently and sweetly. The first story depicts the individuality even of an infant. Nicholas is born with all his potential present, as are all of us, only his is activated rather more quickly. Respect the child! The second is really about doing good by stealth, not wanting to be recognized and praised. Be humble and generous! The third shows how accepting one's individuality and doing acts of kindness leads in the end to sanctity, and that however crushed and annihilated a person may be (cut up and salted for the table), there is always hope, always a chance of being resurrected through someone's prayers. Never despair! The delight of this triptych is its innocent certainty that we shall read the stories aright, and share the artist's joy in them.

Three Legends of St Nicholas **Gerard David** **1500–1510**
Oil on panel   each 55.9 × 33.7cm (22 × 13¼in)
National Gallery of Scotland, Edinburgh

We think of El Greco as a great religious painter, and that is undoubtedly true, but there is sometimes an element of melodrama in his religion which I find off-putting. I feel he is pressuring us towards admiration and emotion, which makes me a little restive. The El Grecos that I can respond to whole-heartedly are his rare and wonderful non-religious works.

One of the very greatest is *Fabula*, meaning 'fable', about the theme of which much learned debate rages. My stab at interpretation is certainly not meant as the final answer, just one of the possible readings to put alongside the others. As I see it, all centres on passion: the fire. In the middle we have youth, a young man, who is blowing on the embers. The act of lighting a candle from a torch has obvious erotic symbolism, and I think we are meant to think of youth encountering the whole marvellous world of sexual adventure. But it is a dangerous world, and he stands between two images of that danger.

We have on one side a man laughing inanely. I see him as indicating one way of misusing passion, not just sexual or erotic passion, but all deep and intense human emotion. This man has lost his wits: he is not a full responsible adult. All our passions can be threatening, and this man avoids their seriousness: he has not matured. On the other side we have the mysterious figure of an ape or monkey, and again there are countless interpretations given. What comes across most clearly to me as its meaning is its unpredictability: we never know what a monkey will do. This is the other danger, that passion can lead us into unpredictable behaviour, our animality in control.

The half-witted man, giggling to himself at the flame, afraid of the serious beauty of passion, and the monkey, driven by desire yet never able to harness it to reality: these two dangers loom threateningly out of the darkness in which this youth must live his life. *Fabula* is saying something vital and intrinsic to every human being, and perhaps I limit it by seeking to give it only one meaning. Just as an image in itself, uninterpreted, it is overwhelming. Perhaps we should keep it open to many meanings and enter the sublime art of El Greco by the doors of the imagination rather than that of the mind. The ideal course is to do both: to experience it at all levels and with all capacities.

Fabula (Fable) **El Greco** c.1585–90
Oil on canvas 66 × 88cm (26 × 34⅝in)
National Gallery of Scotland, Edinburgh

*A*rt is continually full of surprises, and I was absolutely astounded to read that Ruskin, the most famous of Victorian critics, considered Tintoretto a greater artist than Titian. I know Titian well and love him passionately, but I have little knowledge of Tintoretto. Here is one of his greatest works, and seeing it made me understand what Ruskin means. It is a picture, unfortunately cut down at the top, showing Christ being taken down from the Cross, and it bears an enormous emotional weight. But whereas El Greco seems to want to affect the emotions of his audience, what comes across in Tintoretto's painting is the intensity of his own emotions.

He was a tempestuous man, a man of enormous violence and power, and he channelled it all into his art. We become aware of a great surge of disciplined anguish, swirling down from the grieving old head at the top of the picture, along the dead body of Christ, through the pallid looseness of his wounded foot, down through the bending woman until we drop heavily to the horizontal form of the Virgin, lying fainting along the foot of the picture. Such a pressure comes down on her that she almost appears to be dropping right out of sight.

Originally, this painting would have been hung above an altar, and if we do think of her as falling out, she will fall on to the altar and lie there surrendered to her God. But the painting does not stop with 'burial', with descent. It sweeps up again through the other mourning woman, through the energetic back of the sunlit Joseph of Arimathea (or Nicodemus), back to the old man again. Tintoretto makes everything work as a harmonious whole. The bystanders holding candles are not part of the biblical story, but they are so utterly taken up by what is happening that we are taken up with them: they are our stand-ins.

Christ is totally abandoned to deadness, and we are made painfully conscious of it by the contrasting curly head, alive and electric, of the young St John who is carrying the sacred body on his back. It is as if the head has been sundered from the body, a dramatic way of saying that this is an event that will cut John's life in two.

The darkness is shot through with light, glimmering on the bodies, both active and inert, helping us to believe, as the action twists up to the heavens, that grief is not the whole of the meaning. This painting is about an end that is also, triumphantly, a beginning, and the glory of Tintoretto is to make both fully credible. It is a paradox, life from death, but a heavenly paradox. In fact, this is the essential paradox of all great and tragic art, to take what is darkest and transform it into light.

The Deposition of Christ **Jacopo Tintoretto** **c.1550–60**
Oil on canvas 203 × 150cm (79⅞ × 59in)
National Gallery of Scotland, Edinburgh

The Painter's Wife and Anne Bayne, Mrs Allan Ramsay

Allan Ramsay

Born Edinburgh, Scotland 1713
Died London, England 1784

~

It is astonishing how a great artist can seem to be overlooked by history. Allan Ramsay, the Scottish portrait painter of genius, has not been exactly forgotten (especially in his home town, Edinburgh), but he has not yet had full recognition. His masterpiece is the portrait of his second wife, Margaret Lindsay. They eloped together and had to suffer a great deal of parental opposition, but he cherished her dearly, and you can see here that cherishing, that attentive, loving tenderness. She has a strong and beautiful face, turned towards her husband with undisguised affection. He catches so subtly the contrast between the power of her bone structure and the softness of the ribbons and lace that surround her. She has strained back her soft and silky hair, and he paints every strand of it with care.

Opinions differ as to her expression: some see a serene look as her husband enters the room, others have seen an apprehension there. She had nothing to be apprehensive about actually, because we happen to know that she had a long and happy life with him. Their children lived, which was comparatively rare in those days, and right to the end she was the joy of his heart. If there is apprehension, it must be a projection of Ramsay's own feelings. The flowers she is arranging will fade and die, because beauty does not endure. The lovely flower-like woman is fragile too, agonizingly so. Love her as he will, he cannot hold her away from death. The reason for this tremulous sense of our human vulnerability, which gives this portrait its profundity, lies in Ramsay's history. He had lost his first wife, Anne, whom he had also loved very dearly, after only four years of married life together. All three of their children also died, and now Ramsay can never feel secure when painting someone precious to him.

We can see the difference in the two portraits. The picture of Anne is a splendid affirmation of a strong, alert, intelligent woman. She looks at her husband with a kind of a happy cheekiness, so that you can feel she gave as good as she got. Though it is clearly painted with very great attention to her personality, there is not here that note of sensitive tenderness that is so striking in Margaret's portrait. This one is a partner, Margaret is a wife. It was after Anne's death in 1743 that Ramsay passed from being a very good painter into greatness. In the later picture we see that he has lost his innocent belief in the goodness of life; he knows now that for all of us happiness is held on a very loose rein and is not to be possessed for ever.

The Painter's Wife **Allan Ramsay** c.1760
Oil on canvas 76.2 × 63.5cm (30 × 25in)
National Gallery of Scotland, Edinburgh

Anne Bayne, Mrs Allan Ramsay
Allan Ramsay c.1739/43
Oil on canvas 68.3 × 54.7cm (26⅞ × 21½in)
Scottish National Portrait Gallery, Edinburgh

BRIEF LIVES OF THE ARTISTS

Domenico BECCAFUMI (c.1485–1551)

*T*he last great painter of the Sienese school, Beccafumi was heavily influenced by his years in Rome (1510–1512) when Michelangelo was painting the ceiling of the Vatican's Sistine Chapel. His own intentions were more secular, however, and it is no surprise that his greatest commission was to decorate the Palazzo Pubblico in Siena. Beccafumi was perhaps the leading non-Florentine Mannerist, exploring to the full that strange, melodramatic but fascinating art form that was an early sixteenth-century reaction to the far more classical disciplines of Renaissance art.

~

Paul CÉZANNE (1839–1906)

*B*orn in Aix-en-Provence, France, Cézanne desired with a continually deepening passion to become an artist, although his father intended him to be a lawyer and the art establishment in Paris thought him remarkably ham-handed. In 1861 he went to Paris where he entered into the revolutionary fervour of the time with his friend Emile Zola and also applied to the conservative Académie des Beaux Arts. He submitted work to the first Impressionist exhibitions in 1874 and 1877 but his style was not well received. On his father's death in 1886, Cézanne was able to retreat to Provence and devote himself to the revolutionary paintings which were to form the basis of twentieth-century art, though he himself humbly and stubbornly always felt he was falling short.

~

CLAUDE Lorrain(e) (1600–1682)

*C*laude Gellée was born in Lorraine, hence the name by which he is usually known. He began his career in a humble way as a studio assistant though he soon found his own artistic voice. However French he was, Claude, like Poussin, was much happier and more creative in Rome. He painted the Roman countryside in an idealized way, fusing what he saw with the imagined landscapes of the classical past. He made European landscape painting into poetry and his subsequent influence has been immense.

~

Gerard DAVID (?1460–1523)

*D*avid was born in the town of Oudewater in the Netherlands. He trained in Haarlem but worked in Bruges from 1484. He was commissioned by the city, whose commercial influence was on the wane as Antwerp's grew, to paint moralistic paintings warning officials of the punishments for corruption. This makes David sound rather starchy but in fact he was a delightful painter. There was often a touch of humour in his work which gives an added dimension to its emotional qualities. David was extremely popular in his day and his compositions were much copied.

~

Sir Anthony van DYCK (1599–1641)

Although Flemish by birth, van Dyck is perhaps best known as the painter of the English court. He joined the Painters' Guild in Antwerp, where he was born, in 1618 and became chief assistant in Rubens' workshop there. He was a great traveller who moved through the fashionable circles of Italy and the Netherlands, painting the aristocracy as an aristocrat. In 1632 Charles I persuaded van Dyck to come to England where he remained, married and died young.

~

Jan GOSSAERT (c.1478–c.1533)

Born in Maubeuge, Flanders and consequently known as Mabuse, Jan Gossaert worked first in Antwerp and then travelled to Rome in 1508. There the Italian style overwhelmed him and dominated his work for the rest of his life. He seems to have been the first to bring Italian classicism, with its love for the nude, to Flanders, thus uniting the strength of the Flemish Gothic style and the Renaissance elegance of Italy.

~

El GRECO (1541–1614)

Born in Crete, Domenikos Theotokopoulos, El Greco ('the Greek') was mainly active in Spain. He trained in Crete, then a Venetian possession, as an icon painter and always showed the influence of Titian. El Greco came into his own when he settled in Toledo, Spain, in 1577 and the Spanish intelligentsia soon recognized his quality and began giving him regular commissions. The violent upheavals and intense spirituality of the Counter-Reformation fused with Greco's own affinity with Mannerist innovation to create his extraordinary style characterized by its distorted figures and strange, almost mystical, colours. As times changed, his circle of admirers diminished but there were always those who responded to his singularity of vision.

~

Il GUERCINO (1591–1666)

Born Giovanni Francesco Barbieri, Guercino's squint earned him his nickname. Reputed to have painted a fresco of the Madonna on his parents' house when he was eight, Guercino was thought to be something of a prodigy. Since his birthplace, Cento, had little in the way of an artistic tradition he had to look to nearby cities to find patronage. For much of his life, though, Guercino was overshadowed in public esteem by the great Guido Reni in Bologna and hardly left his home town. On Reni's death in 1643, he took over his rival's position, abandoning much of the darkness of his painting for a lighter, more classical style.

~

Jan Davidsz de HEEM (1606–1683)

*O*ne of the very greatest still-life painters, Jan Davidsz de Heem was able to show the amazing potential of this apparently narrow genre. Born in Utrecht, he fled from its religious upheavals to Antwerp in 1636. De Heem's paintings mainly feature fruit, flowers and household objects and are designed to reflect the transience of earthly things. Both his father and his son were still-life painters, but Jan Davidsz was the most successful of the three. He moved back to Utrecht in 1669, returning to Antwerp a couple of years later where he remained until his death.

~

David HOCKNEY (b. 1937)

*D*avid Hockney is probably the most successful living British painter. Born in Bradford, Yorkshire, he studied there until 1957. After two years' National Service as a conscientious objector, Hockney entered the Royal College of Art in London, but it was only when he moved to California that he found his own voice, seen superbly in paintings such as *A Bigger Splash* (1967) and other landscapes of the poolside. During this stage he became increasingly interested in the problems of naturalistic representation in painting, but more recently much of his time has been taken up with photography and stage design.

~

Gerrit van HONTHORST (1590–1656)

*A*lthough born in Utrecht in the Netherlands, Honthorst learned to be a painter in Italy and when he returned home he showed how heavily he had been influenced by Caravaggio. Indeed, so deeply was he immersed in Caravaggio's use of *chiaroscuro*, the interplay of light and dark, that in Italy he was known as Gherardo delle Notti – 'Gerard of the Night'. Honthorst seems to have been highly susceptible to influences and later in his career adopted a more courtly style akin to van Dyck. He painted Charles I with his wife Henrietta Maria and was court painter at The Hague from 1637 to 1652.

~

Jan LIEVENS (1607–1674)

*J*an Lievens was a painter in his own right at the age of 13 and from around 1625 worked extremely closely with Rembrandt in Leyden, in the Netherlands. It seems likely that they shared a studio and used the same models, and they even worked on the same paintings – some works from this period are signed 'Lievens, retouched by Rembrandt'. Rembrandt moved to Amsterdam in the early

1630s and Lievens visited England before moving again to Antwerp. After the split, Lievens seems to have lost ground to his former collaborator, but still managed to maintain a successful career as a painter of portraits and allegories.

~

Filippino LIPPI (1457/8–1504)

The child of Fra Filippo Lippi and Lucrezia Buti's marriage, Filippino Lippi inherited some of his father's gifts. Filippo died when his son was twelve, but he was semi-adopted by Botticelli who both fathered and taught him. So close were they artistically that some works probably by the pair have been attributed to an imaginary third artist, Amico di Sandro (ie, friend of Botticelli), because they cannot with any certainty be ascribed to either. Filippino Lippi developed a uniquely diaphanous style of art which was much admired and led to the prestigious commission to complete Masaccio's fresco cycle in the Brancacci Chapel of Santa Maria del Carmine, ironically where his father had been a monk.

~

Fra Filippo LIPPI (1406–1469)

Orphaned young, Lippi was brought up as a member of a Carmelite friary in Florence where he took his vows (hence the prefix 'Fra', 'Brother'). He had the good fortune to be taught for a short time by Masaccio, the greatest painter since Giotto. At no time however did he choose to be a monk and it was understandable, even to his contemporaries – but nevertheless scandalous – when he eloped with the nun Lucrezia Buti. Fortunately Lippi's artistic talents had earned him the friendship of the powerful Medici family who obtained the dispensation necessary for Lippi and Lucrezia to marry. Though Lippi's reputation, as exemplified in Victorian poet Robert Browning's poem *Fra Lippo Lippi*, is that of a worldly Renaissance man rebelling against the confines of the Catholic Church, the piety of much of his painting seems to belie this. Towards the end of his life, though apparently in ill health, Lippi was Botticelli's tutor.

~

Lorenzo LOTTO (c. 1480–1556)

Lotto's strange and distinctive style attracted commissions from all over Italy. He may have trained with Giorgione and Titian under Giovanni and Gentile Bellini, but few details of his life are certain. Most of Lotto's work is religious in subject but always with a unique slant. He is not exactly subversive, but his interpretations are amongst the most personal in art history. This is perhaps most evident in his portraits. Towards the end of his life, Lotto became a lay brother in a monastery near Loreto, where he later died.

Simone MARTINI (c. 1284–1344)

Although little is known of Simone's early years in Siena, he was probably a pupil of Duccio, the first great Sienese painter. By 1325 Simone had gained sufficient fame to be commissioned to paint a *Maestà* (the Madonna and Child enthroned in glory) in the Palazzo Pubblico, Siena. In 1317 he was summoned to Naples, then a French kingdom, to paint a portrait commemorating the coronation of Robert of Anjou. This was a political commission, but Simone so internalized his theme that he produced a portrait of overwhelming power. Towards the end of his life, he settled in Avignon, the home of the Papacy, where he met, befriended and worked with the poet Petrarch. In his work the lightness, elegance and charm of the Sienese school is at its most enchanting.

~

Dhruva MISTRY (b. 1957)

Dhruva Mistry was born in Kanjari, India, and studied at the University of Baroda before taking an MA at London's Royal College of Art in 1983. His first solo exhibition was in New Delhi in 1981. He was Artist in Residence at Kettle's Yard gallery in Cambridge and an honorary Fellow of Churchill College, Cambridge in 1984–85, and represented Britain at the third Rodin Grand Prize Exhibition in Japan in 1990.

~

PALMA Vecchio (1480–1528)

Born Jacopo Palma, but later called Vecchio – 'the elder' – to distinguish him from his grand-nephew, Palma Giovane, Palma Vecchio was born near Bergamo, Italy, probably trained under Giovanni Bellini and was artistically most active in Venice. Very few further details are known of his life. He is best known as a painter of female figures, usually blonde and voluptuous, at half length or reclining, in vivid colours.

~

PIERO di Cosimo (c. 1462–c. 1521)

Details of the life of this artist of the Florentine school are few. Not many of his works are reliably dated and no signed documents are extant. He may have worked on the frescoes in the Sistine Chapel in the Vatican with his teacher, Cosimo Rosselli. Piero's work is often distinguished by its characteristic and highly imaginative subject matter. Many of his paintings – often of fauns, centaurs or primitive people – seem rather hard to understand at first but it is necessary to look at their mythological background to fully understand his skill.

~

Nicolas POUSSIN (1594–1665)

Poussin, one of the very great painters and certainly the most important French painter of the seventeenth century, actually spent his most productive years in Italy. Born in Normandy, he moved to Paris around 1612 to study and then to Rome in 1624. As his reputation grew, he began to get important commissions, such as painting an altarpiece for St Peter's in Rome, and in 1640 he was summoned back to France by Louis XIII and Cardinal Richelieu. Although he was housed in a wing of the Tuileries palace and made Superintendent of the Academy, Poussin found the artistic climate in Paris stifling and returned to his beloved Rome in 1642 where he remained for the rest of his life. His vision of the landscape, profoundly intellectual while at the same time profoundly romantic, does not always have immediate appeal but there is no painter who more repays close study.

~

Allan RAMSAY (1713–1784)

Allan Ramsay trained in Rome and Naples before settling down to the business of painting portraits in London around 1739. He had taken on board many European styles and ideas which were somewhat ahead of their time – and ahead of those of his chief rival, Joshua Reynolds. However, Ramsay was a man of many gifts and his ambitions as a painter were never enough to stop him enjoying his other pleasures of travel, conversation and literature. Dr Johnson, who delighted in conversation, was never happier than when exchanging views with Allan Ramsay, who also met with many of the great thinkers of the day such as Rousseau and Hume. In the 1760s he was appointed court painter to George III, but an accident to his arm restricted his work as an artist and at the end of his life he became better known as an intellectual and speaker.

~

Pierre Auguste RENOIR (1841–1919)

Renoir's artistic career began in 1854 as a painter in a ceramics factory, something which is reflected in the porcelain gleam which characterizes his best known work. As a student he became friends with Monet and Sisley, the former a poor man like himself, the latter from a more moneyed background. By the late 1860s, Renoir and Monet were developing the techniques of Impressionism, painting *en plein air* around the Seine in Paris and abandoning drawing and outlines in painting in favour of patches of light and dark colours. The Impressionist exhibitions made Renoir's name around the world and he travelled widely, but by 1906 he had settled in Cagnes, France and was badly affected by arthritis. Refusing to admit his physical disabilities, he devoted his last years to sculpture, which he masterminded by directing assistants from his wheelchair.

~

Jusepe de RIBERA (1591–1652)

Born in Spain as José, Ribera became Jusepe when he moved to Naples – at the time a Spanish possession – in 1616. He appears in Byron's *Don Juan* as Spagnoletto, the nickname he was given by the Italians. Many of Ribera's paintings exhibit a violence and an uncompromising realism completely at odds with the ideals of classicism. He painted classical philosophers and biblical figures as beggars and beggars as heroes. Ribera was bowled over by the dramatic light and shade effects of Caravaggio and fused what he saw with his existing skills to create a new style. He had sorrows as he grew older — his daughter was abducted and his health was poor — and he died as much a hero as one of his beloved martyrs.

~

Sir Peter Paul RUBENS (1577–1640)

*R*ubens' career was an uninterrupted success from the time he left his birthplace, Siegen in Westphalia, and moved to Antwerp in 1589. Like many painters of the day, he subsequently went to Italy where the power and beauty of his work was fully recognized and in 1608 he was invited by the Spanish Governors of the Netherlands to return to Antwerp as court painter. Here, Rubens ran a vast studio and employed many assistants — including van Dyck — which meant that his engravings, and so his fame, spread across Europe. He won nearly all the prestigious commissions of his day, including painting the ceiling of Charles I's Banqueting House in Whitehall in London. He was also called upon by the government to act as a diplomat and negotiate treaties, which he did with great success. Rubens was a man of courtly demeanour, tact and great integrity who also had the bliss of an extremely happy private life. Four years after the death of his beloved first wife in 1626 he fell passionately in love with the 16-year-old Hélène Fourment and devoted much of his later life to her.

~

Giovanni Girolamo SAVOLDO (c.1480–c.1550)

*B*orn in Brescia, Italy, but active mainly in Venice, Savoldo's artistic career was neither prolific nor, at the time, particularly successful. However he is now appreciated as a minor master in his own right, particularly for his inventive use of light and dark effects in night scenes, which in many ways prefigures Caravaggio. Savoldo worked in Florence and Milan as well, where the touch of lyricism in his work was particularly appreciated.

~

Cesare da SESTO (1477–1540)

A pupil of Leonardo who was known as 'Le Milanese' (he was born in Milan), very little information is available about da Sesto's life. He seems to have visited Rome and Naples, but da Sesto's importance as an artist derives principally from his association with Leonardo da Vinci. Since we have so few extant works by Leonardo, da Sesto's reworkings — such as his copy of *Leda and the Swan* — form a valuable record of those paintings which have been lost or destroyed.

Sir Stanley SPENCER (1891–1959)

Stanley Spencer is one of the great eccentrics of art, totally unlike anyone else either in his personality or his work. His overwhelming unconventionality belies the conventional start to his career at the Slade in London. His time there was interrupted by the First World War, during which he served in Macedonia. This was an experience that inspired some of his most important works such as the murals on the walls of the memorial chapel in Burghclere, Hampshire. As official war artist during the Second World War he drew his inspiration from the shipyards of Glasgow but it was his home village of Cookham (he called it 'the holy suburb of Heaven') which is the backdrop for his best known canvases such as *Resurrection, Cookham* which he painted in 1926. Spencer's unorthodox theology and views on sexual liberation frequently caused controversy, although he was knighted in 1959 shortly before his death.

~

Jacopo Robusti TINTORETTO (1518–1594)

We have little information on the early life of Tintoretto other than that he was born in Venice. He seems to have aroused a great deal of jealousy, mainly because of the inventive methods he used to win commissions, and to have been a larger-than-life character of enormous energy. He ran a very large workshop employing, amongst others, his two sons and one daughter. Tintoretto would make small wax models of figures and by using spotlights was able to experiment with shadows and composition. His major work is at the Scuola di San Rocco in Venice where he painted a vast series depicting the Life of the Virgin and the Life of Christ.

~

TITIAN (c.1487–1576)

Born Tiziano Vecelli in Pieve di Cadore in the Italian Dolomites, Titian most likely served as an apprentice to both Gentile and Giovanni Bellini, but was perhaps most profoundly influenced by Giorgione. He was the only artist of the day who can be compared in stature to Michelangelo but whereas Michelangelo drew his strength from his association with the Papacy Titian – a much more worldly man – was the court painter to the Holy Roman Emperors. In 1532, Emperor Charles V commissioned him to paint his portrait and a unique relationship developed which continued into the reign of Charles's successor, Philip II of Spain. Titian died of the plague claiming to be 99 but scholars have continually revised his date of birth, assuming that he added a few years to his age in order to boost his prestige.

~

Paolo UCCELLO (1396/7–1475)

According to the biographer Vasari, Paolo di Dono became known as Uccello ('bird') because of his love of birds, which he would free from their cages in the market. He studied in Florence under Ghiberti from 1407 and did mosaic work in St Mark's, Venice for several years in the late 1420s.

When he was introduced to the new mathematical and artistic tool of perspective, he was completely bowled over by it and it increasingly dominated his life and his work. Although Uccello's career involved some highly prestigious commissions, he was not a typical professional artist. Later in his career he lived as a virtual hermit and he seems to have become more eccentric as he aged.

~

Elisabeth VIGÉE-LEBRUN (1755–1842)

Like most women artists, Vigée-Lebrun was only able to be trained because there was an artist in the family – her father. However she outstripped him and achieved great success as a society portraitist in France. Such was her skill and reputation that in 1779 she was summoned to paint Marie-Antoinette, whose confidante she became. She hosted a fashionable salon of her own and became a member of the Academy in 1783. Her rise was interrupted by the French Revolution in 1789 but with her usual skill and intelligence she skipped out of Paris in good time and embarked on a tour of the capitals of Europe. A pretty, ambitious and self-centred woman, Vigée-Lebrun published her memoirs in 1837 which disclose more about herself than she may have realized.

~

PICTURE CREDITS

BBC Books would like to thank the following for providing photographs and for permission to reproduce copyright material. While every effort has been made to trace and acknowledge all copyright holders, we would like to apologise should there have been any errors or omissions.

15, 17, Board of Trustees of the National Museums and Galleries on Merseyside: Walker Art Gallery, Liverpool; 19, Collection of Sir Denis Mahon; 21, Board of Trustees of the National Museums and Galleries on Merseyside: Walker Art Gallery, Liverpool; 23, Board of Trustees of the National Museums and Galleries on Merseyside: Walker Art Gallery, Liverpool, © David Hockney; 25, Fitzwilliam Museum, University of Cambridge, © Estate of Stanley Spencer, 1933, All Rights Reserved DACS; 29, Fitzwilliam Museum, University of Cambridge; 31, By kind permission of the Provost and Scholars of King's College, Cambridge; 33, 35, 37, Fitzwilliam Museum, University of Cambridge; 41, 43, 45, Ashmolean Museum, Oxford; 47, The Governing Body, Christ Church, Oxford; 49, Ashmolean Museum, Oxford; 53, 55, 57, 59, 61, Courtesy of the Earl of Pembroke, Wilton House; 65, 67, 69, 71, 73, The Barber Institute of Fine Arts, The University of Birmingham; 77, 79, 81, 83, National Gallery of Scotland; 85, (left) National Gallery of Scotland, (right) Scottish National Portrait Gallery.

INDEX

Page numbers in *italic* refer to the illustrations

9/93   4GS